M000120647

HOPE

ALSO AVAILABLE FROM BLOOMSBURY

Enduring Time, Lisa Baraitser
Slow Philosophy: Reading against the Institution,
Michelle Boulous Walker

HOPE

The Politics of Optimism

SIMON WORTHAM

BLOOMSBURY ACADEMIC
LONDON • NEW YORK • OXFORD • NEW DELHI • SYDNEY

BLOOMSBURY ACADEMIC
Bloomsbury Publishing Plc
50 Bedford Square, London, WC1B 3DP, UK
1385 Broadway, New York, NY 10018, USA

BLOOMSBURY, BLOOMSBURY ACADEMIC and the Diana
logo are trademarks of Bloomsbury Publishing Plc

First published in Great Britain 2020

Copyright © Simon Wortham, 2020

Simon Wortham has asserted his right under the Copyright,
Designs and Patents Act, 1988, to be identified as Author of this work.

For legal purposes the Acknowledgements on p. vii constitute an
extension of this copyright page.

Cover design by Maria Rajka
Cover image © Dan Krauss / Getty Images

All rights reserved. No part of this publication may be reproduced or
transmitted in any form or by any means, electronic or mechanical,
including photocopying, recording, or any information storage or retrieval
system, without prior permission in writing from the publishers.

Bloomsbury Publishing Plc does not have any control over, or
responsibility for, any third-party websites referred to or in this book. All
internet addresses given in this book were correct at the time of going
to press. The author and publisher regret any inconvenience caused if
addresses have changed or sites have ceased to exist, but can accept no
responsibility for any such changes.

A catalogue record for this book is available from the British Library.

A catalog record for this book is available from the Library of Congress.

ISBN:	HB:	978-1-3501-0529-4
	PB:	978-1-3501-0530-0
	ePDF:	978-1-3501-0528-7
	eBook:	978-1-3501-0531-7

Typeset by Integra Software Services Pvt. Ltd.
Printed and bound in Great Britain

To find out more about our authors and books visit www.bloomsbury.com
and sign up for our newsletters.

CONTENTS

Acknowledgements vii

Hope against hope 1

**TWENTY-TWO SHORT ESSAYS ON THE
POLITICS OF OPTIMISM**

1 Immanuel Kant: Choosing what is best 15

2 Voltaire: Bien (tout est) 21

3 Arthur Schopenhauer: Eating the other 25

4 Benedict de Spinoza: Hope, faith and
judgement 29

5 Friedrich Nietzsche: Imperfect nihilism 35

6 Maurice Blanchot: Hope and poetry 41

7 Jacques Derrida: Yes, yes 45

8 Emmanuel Levinas: Sociality and solitude 51

9 Sigmund Freud: 'A time-consuming business' 59

10 Melanie Klein: 'Therapeutic pessimism' in
Kristeva's view 71

11 Julia Kristeva: 'Psychoanalysis – a counterdepressant' 75

12 Walter Benjamin: 'Pessimism all along the line' 81

13 Theodor Adorno: 'Hurrah-optimism' 85

14 Hannah Arendt: 'The right to expect miracles' 89

15 Slavoj Žižek: Hopeless courage (with Hegel and Badiou) 95

16 Franz Kafka: 'Plenty of hope, an infinite amount of hope – but not for us' (re-reading Walter Benjamin) 103

17 Jacques Derrida: Hegel, Bataille, negativity and affirmation 109

18 Frantz Fanon: Recognition and conflict 117

19 Hannah Arendt: Violence and power 125

20 Étienne Balibar: Politics and psychoanalysis 133

21 Hans Kelsen: Politics and the 'impolitical' 139

22 Sigmund Freud: Super-ego politics 145

Notes 155
Index 168

ACKNOWLEDGEMENTS

Some of the material in this book was originally published as 'Antinomies of the Super-Ego: Etienne Balibar and the Question of the Psycho-Political' in *Philosophy Today*, 61.4 (2017). I am grateful for the permission to reproduce, with a few changes, here.

Hope is traversed by the hatred of others, by resentment.

One could say that hope is not the imaginary of an ideal justice dispensed at last, but what accompanies the patience of truth, or the practical universality of love, through the ordeal of the real … From this point of view, hope has nothing to do with the future.

Alain Badiou, *Saint Paul: The Foundation of Universalism*,
trans. Ray Brassier (Stanford, CA:
Stanford University Press, 2003), 94–97

HOPE AGAINST HOPE

In his 2017 book, *The Courage of Hopelessness*, Slavoj Žižek offers a wide-ranging analysis of what he sees as 'the impasses of global capitalism'[1] and the political, economic and cultural conflicts to which they give rise. Included here are the politics of contemporary international trade agreements, the crisis of Syriza in Greece over the past decade as an expression of the immense question of Europe today, China's 'alternative modernity' and the inadequately understood social and political models it generates, the impact of various religious fundamentalisms on a worldwide scale, the sundry effects of terrorism, security, populism, evolving sexual politics and social media, the continuing rise of anti-capitalist protest and so on. We are treated to a fast-paced, headlong dash through current political events and issues. Like other works by Žižek, the book is as recognizably breathless in its approach as it is extensive in its ambitions and imaginative in the linkages it wishes to make between the themes and objects of analysis. Whether or not Žižek is right to offer up this particular mix is not, however, my main concern. There are undoubtedly many scholars, writers and critics who are better equipped than I am to evaluate, debate and offer challenge on the precise nature of contemporary economic realities, on the nuances of trade and financial systems, on the workings of international politics and security, on the specific impact of constantly mutating religious legacies upon crisis-ridden 'global capitalism' and so forth. What interests me here, rather, is the theoretical standpoint or critical attitude that Žižek feels is called for in the current circumstances.[2] He unashamedly characterizes his book as 'dark', and expresses his preference for a brand of pessimism that – while it is always happy to be surprised – basically expects nothing. It is in this context, indeed, that Žižek takes inspiration from the notion of 'the courage of hopelessness' to which Giorgio Agamben has recently alluded.[3] It is not only because of the serial failures of the left throughout the twentieth century, and not merely in view of the massive 'deadlock' that seems to define our predicament today, that Žižek eschews the 'theoretical cowardice' which, for him, accompanies the dream of an alternative (xi). Rather, hope itself functions as a palliative. Like the reassurance the smoker gives themselves that they will one day quit, it reduces urgency, impeding rather than encouraging immediate change. For Žižek, then, rather than speculating on the promise of a proverbial 'light at the end of the tunnel', we must endure the 'zero point' of hopelessness – the desperate prospect of no imaginable improvement – as the very condition of potential emancipation (x). Žižek's dissatisfaction with leftist optimism is far from new, of course, and indeed represents a particular standpoint that can be traced within the intellectual traditions of the left itself. As long ago as the late 1920s, for instance, Walter Benjamin backed what he saw as surrealism's rejection of the bourgeois intelligentsia's 'well-meaning' left-wing idealism on the grounds that it was utterly sclerotic. In contrast to the shallow, self-serving optimism which characterized this 'moralizing dilettantism', Benjamin advocated 'pessimism all along the line', albeit an organized pessimism that conveyed his own sense of revolutionary possibility.[4] Writing during the Second World War, meanwhile, Theodor Adorno roundly dismissed the 'hurrah-optimism' of those that led the workers' movement in the United States as little more than the conduit of dogmatic blind hope and, to boot, a source of dead-end identification with oppression that demanded solidarity of a suffocating rather than liberating type.[5] And yet, as I suggest in this book, one may detect a modicum of something like hope transecting the antithetical task of thought which Adorno himself contrasts to the business of such 'frantic optimism', as he puts it; just as the hopeless 'courage' of a certain post-Hegelian left may reinvest hopes in the very process of eschewing them.

Arguments concerning the continuing significance and perceived limits of hope for radical leftist thought today are, in many respects, at the heart of this book, and much could be said about the seeming impasse or mismatch between the hugely pessimistic diagnoses of contemporary politics which often prevail today and the optimistic resources of a leftist politics of resistance and transformation that is also a feature of our political landscape. Factored into this equation, of course, would need to be the capacity of post-Trump politics to appropriate, invert or, better, evacuate the meaning of our cultural and political lexicon through an idiomatic performativity recognizable in each of its gestures and acts, creating a political theatre in which supposedly familiar distinctions are merely the resource for highly charged forms of play. Here, what may be pessimistic or optimistic in the first place becomes far from certain, and it is likely that, rather than these terms providing a basis for stable position-taking, one would need to evaluate the very fluid cross-currents that now flow through any interchange they may have, whether that interchange is overt or implicit. Writing during the first decade of the twenty-first century, Lauren Berlant identified a 'cruel optimism' coursing through our relationship to contemporary culture and politics, whereby each of the attachments that we form (inherently optimistic though they may be, whether they feel like it or not) has a habit of confronting possibility with its own more or less immediate limits, so that

increasingly we live in cultural and political environments defined
by 'fraying fantasies' and 'dissolving assurances', leaving us in
a position where 'adjustment' feels like the 'accomplishment' (in
other words, where the 'optimism' of our attachments in fact cruelly
controls and constrains possibility through its very workings).[6]
Written before the advent of Trump and the latest transformations
of 'neoliberal' or 'populist' politics, it would be interesting to debate
the particular forms that such 'cruel optimism' takes today, not
least for a politics of resistance. Berlant's analysis should certainty
prompt further discussion and research as we move towards
the third decade of the twenty-first century.[7] However, it is my
intention to situate hope's ongoing and persistent complexity
not only within the contemporary moment, but also within the
broader context of an intellectual or philosophical legacy handed
down from the Enlightenment onward. That's not to depoliticize
the topic, far from it. But the divided and inconsistent conceptual
resources of those traditions of thought that we may label
optimistic or pessimistic are, I would argue, as influential in shaping
contemporary political perspectives and possibilities as either the
impact of the left's recurrent failure or the seeming prison-house
of current global realities. They cut right across the very possibility
of thinking politics. They constitute the very materials or means of
thought, not least political thought, with which one must reckon
if thinking is to persist – and, following Hannah Arendt perhaps, if
politics itself is to persist.[8]

If, for some, it seems remarkable at first glance that hope is
problematic and indeed double-edged for radical thought – that,
rather than being driven by hope's 'bright side', the radical left
increasingly resorts to a combustible 'zero point' from which utter
despair is converted into liberatory agency – I do not believe it is
sufficient simply to offer reminders of a more desperate revolutionary
tendency that detects the origins of authentic emancipation

only in the very darkest and most extreme circumstances. If a constitutive hesitation between hope and its alternatives marks the inner conflict of leftist thought and practice across a broad spectrum, this book suggests this is also because hope itself has a paradoxical 'modern' history. On the cusp of Enlightenment, for example, Spinoza seeks to discredit hope and fear alike as opponents of good judgement; and yet, in the very text where he makes such an argument, hope is partially recuperated as the agent of judgement's consistency with faith.[9] Hope, in other words, is as essentially true as it is avowedly false. No wonder, then, in the century after Spinoza, that hope's duplicity is written all over Enlightenment optimism and its backlash. It's probably the case nowadays that few without an expert philosophical education would appreciate the fact that Enlightenment optimism – a hugely important feature of eighteenth-century thought – largely cautioned that we should hope for nothing. Leibniz's early eighteenth-century proposition that ours is the best of all possible worlds fired decades of philosophical debate throughout Europe. In the 1750s Kant was moved to defend optimism by tackling the main objections to Leibniz.[10] Nevertheless, he was not prepared to support the notion put forth by many optimists that imperfections in the world are a matter of divine choice, but instead maintained that such flaws are an unavoidable product of freedom's necessity. In the process, however, Kant risks the idea that worldly evils might ultimately undermine the optimal character of God's design, even that the creator may not be able to withstand his own creation. If the inherent conservatism of Enlightenment optimism seemed imperilled by its own inner tensions, Voltaire's *Candide* launched perhaps the most famous and most savage attack on what seemed its callous complacency.[11] The book takes aim at philosophical optimism's cold scholarly detachment from everyday human suffering, and lampoons the theodical attitude which suits the lucky few who are able to escape or overcome human misfortunes (usually at the expense of others). And yet the resistance mounted against optimism in Voltaire's book – epitomized by the deeply pessimistic 'philosopher' Martin who accompanies Candide on his travels – is marked by an attitude of hopelessness that ironically characterizes optimism from the outset. Voltaire skewers optimism as trapped between two versions of itself, both of which not only cast God in a terrible light (He is either impotent or cruel), but which paradoxically suggest the suboptimal character of divinity itself. Nonetheless, this searing attack on optimism risks partaking of perhaps its most fundamental mindset. Yet perhaps the greatest irony of philosophical optimism – as opponents like Voltaire and Schopenhauer suggest – is that it does exactly what hope tends to do: it disappoints. However, when such figures advocate casting off optimism's disappointments, the irony is only compounded. In the mid-1800s, a century after optimism's fiercest debates, Schopenhauer himself writes that by rejecting optimism, 'you will regulate your expectations accordingly, and cease to look upon all [life's] disagreeable incidents, great and small, its sufferings, its worries, its misery, as anything unusual or irregular; nay, you will find that everything is as it should be'.[12] One could not imagine a more ironic echo of optimism's central treatise.

For Nietzsche, writing towards the end of the nineteenth century, pessimism provides the prototype for European nihilism, which for him emerges at the intersection of religious disillusionment with the psychological conditions of contemporary culture.[13] As optimism is wholly swept away by pessimism, the meaning and identity of the latter is constituted only by an internal differentiation in Nietzsche's thought between its 'passive' and 'active' sides, with pessimism's weary, embittered version to be resisted and overcome through the energetic vigour of its counterpart. However, an internal tension also marks this 'active' nihilism, which, as Nietzsche himself notes, should remain goalless as its main goal or tenet, even while its objective is to surpass or replace its disenchanted, aimless other. The quandary of nihilism seems to be its highly unstable and perhaps irresolvable relationship to the 'weak' pessimism that constitutes its prototype. However, in a text written in the 1950s to accompany a new German edition of Nietzsche's works, Maurice Blanchot argues that the meaning of nihilism is that it is, in fact, tied to *being* rather than nothingness.[14] However, through its own self-contradiction in regard to being – 'the being that cannot be negated' – nihilism as the more original if 'impossible' response to being's non-negatability actually offers itself, for Blanchot, as an affirmative limit to the dominant and perhaps implicitly negative operations of modern culture and power. The dramatic shift that Blanchot's text makes possible from negation to affirmation (from 'the No to the Yes') where post- or indeed pre-pessimistic nihilism is concerned may provide a context in which to read a text like Jacques Derrida's 'A Number of Yes',[15] which, through careful treatment of the work of Michel de Certeau, argues that all language, discourse or utterance – whether positive or negative – rests on an originary affirmation. The very condition of possibility of language is that it always already says 'yes' in order to say whatever it might say (including any form of 'no'). This is not to reduce the critical potential of language in the conceptual field or for that matter the resistant potential of various language-practices, far from it. But the complex situation of the 'yes, yes' whereby all language cannot but respond to an originary affirmation once more puts the question of an affirmative limit to the negative conditions of utile power or dominant culture as such. And this, I argue, keeps open the question of our response – including our political response – to whatever may be. The point of these examples is that they emerge from what we might term a post-Nietzschean tradition so as to move us somewhat beyond the bare alternatives of optimism or pessimism (whose inner tensions, contradictions and uncanny resonances we have already begun to trace), towards a different thinking of the critical or resistant potentiality of a certain affirmation. Such issues are explored throughout this book, for example in a detailed reading of *Time and the Other* by Emmanuel Levinas, where the rejection of a certain 'optimistic constructivism' that defines the mid-twentieth-century left – with its politics of the 'side-by-side' – is rejected in favour of an affirmation of the constitutive solitude which results from the positing of human existence as distinct from the impersonal *il y a*, the general and unending irremissibility of being.[16] For Levinas, however, this solitude not only represents the freedom and materiality of the existent being, but also places it in a profound relation to death as absolute 'other' which actually comes to *pluralize* existence. Somewhat paradoxically, then, the solitude of existence establishes the very possibility of pluralization in regard to the other, through a radical face-to-face relation that, for Levinas, remains absent in the (optimist–constructivist) 'side-by-side'. If we've already tracked the disenchantment felt by writers like Benjamin and Adorno with superficial and sclerotic forms of leftist solidarity, where certain types of unity become more constraining than they are liberating, the fact that pluralization is accomplished for Levinas in the face of the other, and not by means of a commonality established through the 'side-by-side', asks us to reconsider not only the supposed opposition between 'solitude' and 'sociality' but also the basis on which 'optimism' and 'pessimism' are partitioned more generally. *Time and the Other* calls us to rethink the glib pairing of solitude with pessimism and sociality with optimism, in other words.[17]

In one of his last psychoanalytic texts, Freud recalls the misplaced and premature optimism of 1920s America as a part of an era of hope and prosperity in which quick-fix analytic treatments perhaps inevitably flourished, even though they declined just as quickly as the post-war zeitgeist.[18] In contrast, the seemingly never-ending misery of inter-war Europe, while not exactly a source of nostalgia, provides for Freud a more compelling metaphor for the time-consuming and perhaps interminable task of psychoanalysis. Like a fragile and unsatisfactory peace, one can never know when psychoanalysis will come to an end, and whether its termination will be for good or ill. It is hard to parcel out the optimistic and pessimistic elements of Freud's thinking about psychoanalysis, whether in terms of the analytic treatment of individuals over time or in view of the larger question of psychoanalysis's duration and maturity in the long term. In short, the perhaps interminable nature of psychoanalytic practice is at once a source of despair and hope for Freud: despair, because as analysis goes on, it is never quite clear whether the confrontation between the persistent illness and its curative treatment serves the latter or the former, giving rise as it does to an intensifying brinkmanship that is difficult to calculate; hope, because even if the ailment proves congenital, the interminable character of analysis nonetheless seems to create the very possibility of a future (again, whether for good or ill) which at the very least counters a certain dread of termination. The question of the 'end' or 'ends' of analysis therefore becomes enormously embroiled in this ambivalent and undecidable self-reflection – not only on Freud's part, but for psychoanalysis in general. If Freud's own therapeutic pessimism gives rise to interminable analysis which itself limits or at any rate transforms pessimism in certain respects, Julia Kristeva's reading of Kleinian psychoanalysis at once radicalizes such pessimism, and yet at the same time – perhaps turning pessimism inside out – suggests that psychoanalysis itself may be ventured only in the most radically uncertain and anxious of senses.[19] Kristeva's own *Black*

Sun, meanwhile, suggests ways in which, beyond pessimism about its own practical effectivity, psychoanalysis may serve as a 'counterdepressant' of sorts.[20]

The politics and political possibilities of psychoanalysis come to the fore towards the end of this book. In an important essay by Étienne Balibar, the 1920s debate between Freud and Hans Kelsen over the political import of a psychoanalytic conception of the super-ego is re-examined.[21] Kelsen's intervention, Balibar suggests, leads Freud to significantly reframe his conception of a psychoanalytic 'supplement' of politics. My own reading not only explores Balibar's thinking and writing concerning the possible connections between psychoanalysis and politics, but revisits Freud's *The Ego and the Id* in its own right in order to further pursue Balibar's idea of the antinomic forces at work where politics meets the 'psychoanalytic'. If we are called upon, here, to weigh the hopes of the political from a psychoanalytic point of view, then the sections of the book that precede it act as something of a counterpart suite. They do so, in the sense that – by drawing on key texts by Derrida, Arendt and Frantz Fanon that circulated and intersected in particular ways during the late 1960s – pressing questions are asked about violence and politics. With Fanon very much in her sights, Arendt, in an important essay published in *The New York Review of Books*, specifically questions the inherent connection that was often assumed at the time between violence and power.[22] Instead, she characterizes upsurges of 'political' violence as evidence of power's disintegration rather than its intensification. In turn she disputes the effectiveness of violent resistance as a form of political action, and dismisses the hopes placed in it. However, I argue that Arendt's image of Fanon is questionable from the point of view of an alternative reading offered by 'early' deconstruction of questions of violence and politics in Hegel, which I believe casts Fanon's writing – indebted to Hegel as it is, as much as to psychoanalysis – in a somewhat different light. If, by putting these three authors together, in however uncomfortable or unlikely a way, this part of the book evaluates both the declared limits and the possible reconception of political 'violence', it also seeks to rethink the 'political' from a perspective that complicates as much as restores hope. In both these movements of the book, in other words, we are in the midst of something like hope against hope where the 'political' is concerned[23] – one that resonates, in my view, with the radical venturing of psychoanalysis in Klein, or with Blanchot's remarks on poetry in 'The Great Refusal',[24] with 'the right to expect miracles' beyond all possible hope (post-Hiroshima) in Arendt's *The Promise of Politics*,[25] and with Benjamin's reflections on Kafka's famous phrase 'plenty of hope … but not for us' which for him may be as potentially liberating as it seems radically pessimistic.[26] All of these strange affirmations, or what we might call 'leaps'[27] (each explored further in this book), take us beyond the false alternatives of optimism or pessimism, breaking their deadlock through powerful forms of thinking that, to my mind, do considerable justice to the complexly entangled resources that each has to offer. And I suspect the situation of contemporary politics demands it.

TWENTY-TWO SHORT ESSAYS ON THE POLITICS OF OPTIMISM

1

IMMANUEL KANT

CHOOSING WHAT IS BEST

Two years before it was to be judged, the Prussian Royal Academy chose for their 1755 prize-essay competition the theme of Pope's optimism. While Kant himself decided not to compete, submissions from Lessing, Mendelssohn and Reinhard (who was eventually to win) testify to the currency of debates concerning this topic throughout the cultural and intellectual world of the German Enlightenment. It was Leibniz's *Theodicy*, appearing in 1710, that chiefly fuelled these debates. While in England the optimism of Shaftesbury and Pope had taken its own course during the first half of the eighteenth century, Leibniz's contention that this was the best of all possible worlds had provoked strong criticism, both in France by Bayle and Le Clerc and in Germany by Wolff, Daries and Crusius. Essays submitted to the Prussian Royal Academy for the 1755 prize were supposed to examine Pope's cognate dictum, 'everything is good'. Authors were asked to properly elucidate its meaning and significance, notably in terms of the wider climate of contemporary philosophy, and to establish the grounds for either a philosophical justification or rejection of Pope's position.

The deep resonance of such debates throughout Europe at this time is confirmed by the fact that their intensity grew in response to current events. For example, the question of optimism powerfully funded reactions to the occurrence of natural

disasters such as the Lisbon earthquake, which happened during
the very same year that the prize-essay competition was to be
judged. Faced with the terrible destruction of the town and most
of its inhabitants, Voltaire was moved to abandon optimism. He
savages the Leibnizian world view in his poem on the Lisbon
disaster, which concludes that Leibniz's divine creator falls short
because as the architect of an already optimal world he denies
flawed humanity the very possibility of hope. Widely regarded as a
stepping stone to Voltaire's *Candide* and his view of the problem
of evil (Lisbon also features in Voltaire's picaresque novel), the
poem is brutally critical of optimistic philosophy. While Rousseau
had written to Voltaire to contest his position on the subject, Kant
had reacted to the earthquake by writing three short texts which
challenged the view that philosophical optimism was incompatible
with the incidence of such events.

Reinhard's prize-winning entry, which allied Pope to Leibniz
in its criticism of the optimist position, fired more controversy
and polemic as the unsuccessful entrants rallied against him,
Mendelssohn and Lessing joining forces to malign the idea that
Pope's literary brand of optimism was worthy of comparison
to Leibnizian philosophy in their essay 'Pope a Metaphysician!'
Meanwhile, in 1759 – the year *Candide* appeared – Kant decided,
as he had done in previous years, to announce his lecture
course by appending details to a short text on subject-matter
presumably chosen to cultivate an audience: this time, a defence
of Leibniz's proposition that ours is the best of all possible worlds.
This publication, entitled 'An Attempt at Some Reflections on
Optimism',[1] no doubt prompted by texts and events in the wake of
1755, in turn provoked hostile reaction as another scholar, Daniel
Weyman, misconstrued its contents as a direct attack on his own
recently completed thesis on the topic, publishing a fierce attack
on Kant within days its appearance (one Kant chose to ignore).

Kant begins his essay with the apparently simple idea that 'if God chooses, he chooses only what is best' (71), but makes it clear from the outset that his intention is to re-establish optimism by tackling the main objections to Leibniz's thesis. This defence happens on two fronts. First, Kant refutes as 'erroneously employed' recourse to the mathematical idea of number, whereby the greatest possible figure imaginable can always be increased by addition, which allows its proponents to dispute the Leibnizian contention that this is the best of all possible worlds: on the mathematical parallel, of course, there could always be a better one. Since from this perspective the notion of the greatest possible number is effectively incoherent or 'self-contradictory', so by analogy is that of the most perfect world. If such arguments imply the prospect of possible and perhaps necessary improvement – as Kant puts it, 'a constantly continued and ever possible augmentation' which one might suggest drove a great deal of both philosophical and political thought in the centuries to come – Kant argues instead that the finite nature of the world should be understood less in terms of privation or lack, than in terms of an essential distinction through which only God is infinite. Leibniz's thesis should, thus, be tested according to the degree of 'reality' of our world. The world as by definition 'determinate' must of necessity appear limited if viewed through the mathematical lens, whereas 'the disparity between infinite reality and finite reality is fixed by means of a determinate magnitude which constitutes their difference' and indeed establishes the concept of God (74). Hence, the finite nature of the real world – or, rather, world as 'real' – does not provide the grounds to reject Leibniz's thesis.

Second, Kant dismisses the argument which predicates the theoretical possibility of parallel worlds of equal perfection. Faced with this prospect, one would struggle to make the case that our world was indeed the best of all possible worlds. However, Kant argues that worlds could only be distinct and discrete on condition that their degree of perfection or 'reality' differs, otherwise in effect they would be the same world. From this point of view, therefore, the theoretical postulation of other worlds serves to reinforce rather than undermine arguments about the best world possible.

These technical philosophical refutations of the principal objections to Leibniz are followed in the last pages of the essay by a much simpler and less 'scholarly' justification of optimism on Kant's part. A most perfect world is possible because it is real, or in other words because it has been realized. This realization is a matter of choice, its existence testament to a perfect divinity. If the limitations of our world – for instance, the evils that derive from human freedom – actually attest to its deeper reality as 'the best of schemes', Kant feels able to write in conclusion that '*the whole is the best, and everything is good for the sake of the whole*' (76). If freedom is maintained, here, as both an essential good and a worthy justification of worldly limits, it is also, somewhat paradoxically, just the kind of the necessary 'flaw' that constrains any desire to seek change or improvement to the whole 'scheme' of things. Some might argue, today, that Kant's decision to detach optimism from the prospect of 'a constantly continued and ever possible augmentation' implies a lack of ambition on his part about collective human betterment; here, it would doubtless be telling that the preservation of individual freedom itself implies a certain inertia, politically speaking. Meanwhile, Pope's 'Essay on Man' – perhaps the most notable expression of the optimism which the 1755 prize-essay competition sought to investigate – famously argues that if the reader were only to grasp the bigger picture, order, balance, harmony and reason would be seen to prevail. 'The bliss of man' is 'not to act or think beyond mankind', concludes Pope, since 'man's as perfect as he ought'. 'One truth is clear', he writes at the end of the poem's first epistle: 'Whatever is, is right'.

In an earlier text from 1753, one of three short reflections on optimism that were no doubt prompted by the Prussian Royal Academy's announcement, Kant had succinctly defined Leibnizian optimism as 'the doctrine which justifies the existence of evil in the world by assuming that there is an infinitely perfect, benevolent and omnipotent original being' and 'in spite of all the apparent contradictions, that which is chosen by this infinitely perfect being must nonetheless be the best of all that is possible' (78). Interestingly, in this fragment Kant acknowledges that necessary evils derived from the granting of human freedom may 'in the end spoil even the best plan' (79): if there might be change to this most perfect of possible worlds, it would never be for the better but only for the worse. Good cannot overcome evil in this world, due to freedom's necessity; but evil, it seems, may nevertheless overcome good. In the last text of this triumvirate, however, Kant criticizes Leibnizian optimism for suggesting that god wishes imperfections in the worldly scheme of things, rather than simply accepting them as necessary – the world is not simply a matter of god's pleasure, and it is certainly not his plaything, Kant insists (82–83). There is even the suggestion, here, that god may not be able to withstand his own creation. Man's freedom as a critical feature of the present world seems almost unmatched by divine choice as it confronts its own limitations. If his response to Leibniz and optimism in general seems not entirely free of ambivalence, in later life Kant was purportedly keen that his writings on the subject fell out of circulation. One is left to imagine why.

Nowadays, we tend to think of optimism in terms of the notion that things might improve. Even Pope in his 'Essay on Man' ventures the idea that, knowing god's goodness, we might 'hope humbly' for a blissful afterlife, even if in this best of all possible worlds we must expect no better. But this same tension in Pope's poem establishes hope's predicament for eighteenth-century optimism. The optimist of the Enlightenment world is perhaps the pessimist of the world that comes after it, epitomizing as they do an ingrained conservatism which those seeking positive change must surely overcome.

2

VOLTAIRE

BIEN (TOUT EST)

While the original plan for Voltaire's *Dictionnaire philosophique* took shape during the early 1750s, the first edition was not printed until 1764, when it met with popular enthusiasm but also strong condemnation from civil and religious authorities as a profane and revolutionary book.[1] In the meantime, in 1759 Voltaire's picaresque novel *Candide, ou l'Optimisme*, was published, gaining notoriety across Europe as a scandalous work of blasphemy and sedition.[2] Tutored in Enlightenment philosophy from the vantage point of a comparatively idyllic life in Germanic Westphalia, the protagonist Candide suffers a series of misfortunes which drive him haphazardly across the war-torn and crisis-ridden geopolitical landscape of eighteenth-century Europe, and indeed beyond. In the process, his philosophically cultivated optimism is profoundly challenged by a litany of ills of the day. Faced by the worst human miseries, often on an epic scale, philosophical debate itself is presented in *Candide* as narrowly pedantic and indulgent, mostly a self-regarding exercise in scholarly erudition and inevitably a futile interlude in the otherwise relentless onslaught of human misfortune. Where the good life does exist – albeit in the fantastical lost country of El Dorado stumbled on by Candide during his many travels and adventures, where the denizens enjoy long-life, justice, peace, happiness, tolerance and wealth – it is far from a part of the best possible world for all, but is instead the insular preserve of a privileged minority, without connection or influence in the wider sweep of seemingly inexorable human suffering. (Such a depiction, of course, carries heightened political charge.) While Candide's confrontation with the most appalling human agonies eventually leads him to renounce optimism in the face of life's realities, nevertheless – and tellingly – he begins to revert when improvements occur in his own situation, albeit they come at the price of unwarranted suffering on the part of others. Optimism's quasi-theodical tendency is indeed to retroactively reinterpret terrible events in terms of an ultimately beneficial outcome, whereby the turmoil and torment suffered by many along the way are utterly disregarded. Equally, even those human misfortunes in *Candide* which might be regarded as just punishment of the high or mighty usually involve senseless pain and misery for others – usually the poor and vulnerable in their charge. Meanwhile, the deeply pessimistic 'philosopher' Martin whom the disillusioned Candide selects as his travelling companion (so chosen, because he is the most wretched and dissatisfied of all individuals) struggles to invoke hope – the missing element of Enlightenment optimism – without irony and despair, and is ultimately resigned to the ubiquity of evil, as if nothing could ever get better. Indeed, perhaps the most troubling feature of Voltaire's *Candide* is that opposition or resistance to optimism often partakes of its most salient features.

Meanwhile, in one of the short essays making up Voltaire's *Dictionnaire philosophique*, 'Bien (tout est)' – 'All is good' – we find another sustained attack on optimism. Leibniz is lampooned as an indulged, inward-looking scholar so concerned with philosophical argumentation that he remains unresponsive to real suffering in the world. In contrast, Voltaire quotes the third- and fourth-century church father Lactantius Firmianus, for whom Epicurus argues as follows:

Either god wants to remove the evil from the world, and cannot, or he can, and does not want to; or he neither wants to nor can; or he wants to and can. If he neither wants to nor can, this is impotence, which is contrary to the nature of god; if he can but does not want to, this is wickedness, which is no less contrary to his nature; if he neither can nor wants to this is at once wickedness and impotence; if he wants to and can (which is the only of these possibilities fitting for god) whence comes the evil which is on earth? (69)

Of these different possibilities, let us recall, optimism remains poised between the idea of a god who is simply unable to dispense with evil because of the necessity of earthly freedom (this is Kant's position in one of his 1753 texts on the subject); and the image of a god who, in arriving at the worldly plan which most pleases him, chooses evil as part of a balanced order in the great scheme of things (Kant's criticism of Leibniz in the same text takes aim at this view, but it is also a standpoint that in his *Dictionnaire philosophique* Voltaire associates with Shaftesbury, Bolingbroke and Pope). Is it that god would wish to bring evil to an end, but just can't? This suggests that his powers are limited. Or is it that he doesn't want to, even though he could? This implies wickedness on god's part. While Voltaire observes that quotation is to be avoided as 'usually a ticklish job', here reference to Lactantius exposes the shortcomings of the optimist position as it hesitates between two versions of itself, both of which imply a notion of god that falls short of the original idea of divine power and perfection suffusing all creation. Optimism, in other words, can only resolve its own philosophical difficulties by resorting to an image of god which proves inadequate in terms of optimism's very point of departure. Thus, it is as divided as the god it champions.

In his 1753 text on optimism, where the critical note is sounded in relation to Leibniz, Kant as we've seen goes so far as to hint that god may not survive his own creation, so beleaguered is he by the problem of evil. If one might be tempted to see in Kant's predicament the embryo of the philosophical proposition that god is dead, the alternative idea highlighted by Voltaire – that 'the author of nature' is simply 'a powerful and maleficent king' (73), wholly disdainful of the suffering masses – explains those attacks on his philosophical dictionary that were prompted by its revolutionary flavour as much as its profanity. Indeed, Voltaire's dismantling of the optimist point of view is undertaken more to invite outrage at its deep callousness, than to expose its insidious contradictions. Indeed, such outrage is provoked on behalf of an 'unthinking mass' not schooled in grandiloquent intellectual exercises, those who bear the brunt of worldly sufferings treated as merely a theodical problem by learned proponents of a complacent optimism. Yet in *Candide*, let us recall, the rejection of optimism involves a certain ambivalence as much as clear-cut opposition, not least through the figure of the pessimist philosopher Martin who struggles to find the grounds on which optimism might be surpassed. To confront the best with the worst of all possible worlds may not alter the terms of debate as much as Voltaire hoped, if 'hope' was indeed his aim.

3

ARTHUR SCHOPENHAUER

EATING THE OTHER

In Schopenhauer's short essay 'On the Sufferings of the World', from the last decade of his life, optimism is dismissed as merely the preserve of university professors, once again being seen as an intellectual exercise confined to a learned elite.[1] The essay, appearing several decades after the original publication of *The World as Will and Representation* in the earlier part of the nineteenth century,[2] builds on the sentiment found in this major work by Schopenhauer regarding the optimistic world view, where he famously declares:

> For the rest, I cannot here withhold the statement that *optimism*, where it is not merely the thoughtless talk of those who harbor nothing but words under their shallow foreheads, seems to be not merely an absurd, but also a really *wicked*, way of thinking, a bitter mockery of the unspeakable suffering of mankind. (326)

'On the Sufferings of the World' sees Schopenhauer write that 'evil is positive', explicitly reversing Leibniz's formulation. Since 'misfortune in general is the rule', for Schopenhauer the incidence of what is good merely negates the natural or essential condition of things, of which it is far from the dominant or primary characteristic:

> Every state of welfare, every feeling of satisfaction, is negative
> in its character; that is to say, it consists in freedom from pain,
> which is the positive element of existence. (7)

Nothing gives pause to 'the will to live which underlies the whole world of phenomena'. Such 'will' is incapable of denying itself in the interests of 'redemption', but must 'satisfy its cravings by feeding upon itself' (10).[3] Thus, Schopenhauer writes:

> The pleasure in this world, it has been said, outweighs the pain;
> or, at any rate, there is an even balance between the two. If the
> reader wishes to see shortly whether this statement is true, let
> him compare the respective feelings of two animals, one of
> which is engaged in eating the other. (5)

Confidence in the optimistic standpoint, whether concerning the primacy of good or a balanced order of things, is for Schopenhauer utterly devastated by the 'will' that establishes an absolutely dissymmetrical relationship between satisfaction and suffering, the one being completely dwarfed by the other. Suffering is not in the greater interest of an ultimate 'good', as the optimist would have it; instead, each and every satisfaction of the 'will' (itself an ominously endless pursuit) is bought at an ultimately enormous and unjustifiable price. In the second volume of *The World as Will and Representation*,[4] Schopenhauer remarks that the 'will-to-live' understood as 'the real author of the world' in fact finds its mirror image in the philosophical optimism which, as an uncanny double, offers the will 'unwarranted self-praise' (584). In *Candide*, despite the corrosive effect of life's sufferings, the protagonist's optimism is, ironically, somewhat revived when horrific and calamitous events lead to personal benefits. Optimism, in other words, only endorses the conclusion Schopenhauer draws from the prospect of animals eating each other: any benefits in life are just the consequence of a world of suffering that hugely outweighs them. Thus, for Schopenhauer optimism is both a 'false' and 'pernicious' doctrine, since it effectively licenses the will by sanctioning worldly miseries through the most shallow and misleading of justifications.

'On the Sufferings of the World', meanwhile, establishes a pivotal distinction between human and animal life, whereby animals are less susceptible to acute or protracted suffering, being 'much more content with mere existence' (which also makes them less amenable to 'joy'), whereas 'the life of man' is beset by heightened levels of 'care and anxiety'. For Schopenhauer, the source of this misery is 'hope'. Free from 'care', the animal hopes for nothing. Hope stirs pleasurable anticipation in the human heart, only to sharpen the inevitable agony of subsequent failure or disappointment. (Eaten up by false hope, one might say the human devours itself.) From this point of view, to the extent that it minimizes the chances of hope, proclaiming our world to be optimal in a fundamental or prior sense, the philosophical optimism of Leibniz or Pope would presumably aim to lessen as much as ignore suffering – except that this would perhaps constitute a level of aspiration somewhat at odds with optimism's own disinclination to hope. Optimism gives comfort, in its rhetoric as much as its arguments, paradoxically by subtracting hope from the equation; but by offering such succour as a philosophical or literary selling-point, it not only peddles a reassuring world view to its audience, but perhaps betrays its own ambitions in the process (in other words, its own hopes for itself). Schopenhauer doesn't say as much, but like Voltaire his writing exposes a critical fault line in the optimist position. For every purveyor of optimism's self-satisfactions, there is almost inevitably a reader of *Candide* left all the more despairing in optimism's wake. Despite itself, then, optimism does exactly what Schopenhauer says that 'hope' does. It disappoints. Historically speaking, if nothing else, its initial consolations only compound dissatisfaction and whet outrage at human suffering.

Schopenhauer's profound pessimism leads him to advocate, in this essay, a degree of acquiescence that matches the hopeless resignation of Martin the philosopher in Voltaire's *Candide*. He writes:

> If you accustom yourself to this view of life you will regulate your expectations accordingly, and cease to look upon all its disagreeable incidents, great and small, its sufferings, its worries, its misery, as anything unusual or irregular; nay, you will find that everything is as it should be. (13)

Once more, pessimism rejects optimism's olive branch only to recreate its paradoxical promise almost verbatim: accept your lot as hopeless, and you can at least hope to feel better. By seeking effectively to negate the 'will', such pessimism – aligned by Schopenhauer with a Christian asceticism – adopts a somewhat aspirational position at just the point it advocates acquiescence and self-denial. Given Schopenhauer's own characterization of the all-consuming ferocity of the 'will', hopes of the latter would seem to be decidedly over-optimistic, even if expressed as a form of self-annihilation or self-eating. Since pessimism and optimism would appear to live off as much as eat one another, such dreams of utter destruction are perhaps as paradoxical as the promise that either purveys.

4

BENEDICT DE SPINOZA

HOPE, FAITH AND JUDGEMENT

Before the paradoxes of Enlightenment optimism and its backlash fully emerged, it is possible to see the ambivalent nature of hope taking shape in the work of another thinker, in a way we must surely consider important in regard to its own philosophical posterity. In the opening section of his preface to the 1670 *Theological-Political Treatise*, Spinoza characterizes hope and fear less as different and opposite attitudes of mind, than as the twinned offspring of judgement's lack.[1] In other words, fear and hope alike are the products of a situation in which the proper judgement needed to regulate human affairs is sorely missing, creating a void that is, for Spinoza, inevitably filled by superstitious feelings and ideas based on unsubstantiated belief rather than reasoned thought. Only spurious interpretations of human life and experience derive from our tendency to resort to fear or hope, rather than judgement in a proper sense, in order to make sense of the world. When things go well, we quickly become complacent and thus unreceptive to any form of guidance or advice. But when they go badly, we rush hastily to the nearest available source of assistance and counsel, however ill-considered it may be. We react to life's continual vagaries through wild and unreflective recourse either to desperate supplication or blind sanguinity. Hope and fear are no better – or worse – than one another, to the extent that each operates similarly to prevent judgement taking full hold.

And yet hope and fear are apparently not just the same thing. Within the space of only a few paragraphs, we are told by Spinoza that it is dread that causes irrationality, and that fear is the root of superstition. It is because he is frightened by the prospect of poor fortune or an unhappy fate that Alexander the Great gives way to his superstitious tendencies, and resorts to soothsayers and seers. Such behaviour dwindled when events caused him to become more hopeful. For Spinoza, countless similar examples prove that credulity holds sway when people are afraid. Fear it is that allows religion and government to exert manipulative control, and to shackle liberty. Banishment of fear is therefore a vital precondition of the possibility of free judgement; the seductive and distorting endurance of hope as a potential threat to such joyful emancipation is suddenly overlooked. What causes hope to be effectively decoupled from fear as the counterpart enemy of judgement, when its similar nature seemed so vital to the opening philosophical gambit of Spinoza's treatise? How could this happen so rapidly in Spinoza's prefatory text? (Later on, in fact, the instability or perhaps rather unwarranted prospect of this gesture is somewhat exposed when the interplay between hope and fear is recuperated by Spinoza as he resorts once more to the motif of their close partnership in driving human responses in similar ways.)

Spinoza continues his preface with a lengthy explanation of the causes of judgement's deficit or decline. Divine faith has been corrupted by worldly religion, which is in fact to blame for shrouding doctrine and scripture in inscrutable mysteries that exploit human credulity, rather than offering reverent insight susceptible to good sense and critical appreciation. By this means, scripture is – in the name of religion – merely assented to rather than understood. Whereas, for Spinoza, scripture in its deepest sense actually leaves reason absolutely free (even though the revelation of God's word commands obedience precisely as an expression of faith's true judgement – a seeming paradox that sets the scene for Spinoza's arguments about the compatibility of individual liberty with the stability of the state and sovereign authority). In other words, faith itself is not a matter of superstition, on the contrary, at least not until the fear practised by religion enters the scene. In fact, judgement and faith – when freed from religious or superstitious dread – complement each other entirely. Indeed, one might be tempted to say that they are actually the same thing.

And yet one may suspect that faith, in a certain respect, must also retain a distinctive quality as, precisely, faith. In the chapter of the treatise which elucidates the meaning of faithfulness, obedient faith is not incompatible with individual judgement, far from it. Scripture does not demand, nor even invite, rigid – fearful – adherence to a single, fixed interpretation or understanding, even if the faithful must without exception subscribe to certain basic truths without which obedient devotion is impossible. True faith, in other words, demands piety as much as 'truth' in the sense of conformity to accurate interpretation of given meaning. The person who advances the best reasons for faith is perhaps lesser than the one who demonstrates obedience through acts of charity or justice. Put differently, while divine faith is wholly compatible – and perhaps even coterminous – with judgement in the sense it acquires from the beginning of Spinoza's text, it is far from the simple counterpart of mere 'philosophical' judgement. Unlike theology, the latter is not wedded to obedience or piety, but only 'truth' in a more narrow sense; more narrow, since in the realm of faith, truth is itself thoroughly reliant upon pious devotion, and could not be what it is without such reverence. In other words there is a form of judgement, one that goes the way of 'philosophy', which must be supplemented by piety, indeed suffused with it, in order to acquire consistency and indeed equivalence with faith itself.

But what is it that transforms conceptual judgements of the kind offered by philosophy into this deep amalgam of judgement and faith? Merely piety as an expression of obedience to God? Elsewhere in the treatise, Spinoza reflects on the question of dutiful observance of the law as an expression of freedom. He writes: 'In any form of state the laws should be so drawn up that people are restrained less by fear than hope of something good which they very much desire; for in this way everybody will do his duty willingly' (74). Obedience given freely – obedience, that is, which remains consistent with the judgement of the faithful rather than merely of the philosopher – requires, so it seems, a modicum of hope. Here, indeed, hope is almost the glue that keeps obedience, judgement and faith together (even if hope itself is not totally decoupled in Spinoza's language or phrasing from the restraint imposed by fear, in the sense that the people are 'restrained less by fear than hope of something good'). If faith results from a combination of judgement and obedience which, however, mistrusts thoughtless or exploitative fear, hope remains somewhat the agent of their felicitous interaction. Indeed, Spinoza ends this chapter of his work explicitly devoted to the question of faith with precisely the 'hope' that any 'abuses' of the topic may one day be corrected, not least through the contribution that his own text has made. The revelation of faith, it seems, requires once more a critical modicum of hope.

The separation of hope from fear, as we have seen, threatens to run contrary to the inaugurating move of Spinoza's own treatise, and at times he seeks to recuperate their equivalence. Since, at a certain moment in its arguments, the text also confronts the question of what it may mean to fear God wisely – a question which tolerates fear, as it were, within the ambit of faith and judgement – it is clear that their partition may not be an entirely decisive one. And yet, despite the opening words of Spinoza's treatise, hope cannot be dismissed as contrary to judgement, since pious rather than merely 'philosophical' judgement depends on faith, whose demand for obedience as much as free judgement seems to need a certain amount of hope. Hope, in other words, is both false and true.

5

FRIEDRICH NIETZSCHE

IMPERFECT NIHILISM

For Nietzsche, writing in the 1880s, the onset of nihilism finds its prototype in contemporary forms of pessimism that result from disillusionment with Christian values. 'The sense of *worthlessness* arises when it is understood that the general character of existence does not admit of interpretation in terms of the notions *"purpose"*, *"unity"* or *"truth"*' (19), he writes in the first book of *The Will to Power*, aptly titled 'European Nihilism'.[1] Inherited values connect religious disappointment to the psychological conditions of nihilism. Inspiring guilt/debt, *ressentiment*, and a slavish morality in decline, they seem destined to lead from this growing sense of worthlessness (both of 'man' and the 'world') to pessimistic attitudes that in turn encourage not only loss of faith but also an intensifying nihilistic denaturing of all values. Christian optimism (post-Leibniz) embodied in the notion of the world 'as *perfect*, despite all sorrow and evil, because it included freedom' (15) endowed evil itself with meaning, so that nothing was left outside of its system of values. In the process of devaluing all values, nihilism fully adopts this absence of an 'outside' in the interests of an absolute inversion: in Nietzsche's text, therefore, there is no counterpart or alternative to pessimism as the harbinger of nihilism. Instead, as if to differentiate itself (however unlikely the prospects of self-differentiation might seem), pessimism is marked by its own internal division. Unable to pair with an opposite, it doubles with itself. At its most anarchic or nihilistic, pessimism may be considered a 'sign of strength', but equally when taking the form of 'cosmopolitan dilettantism' brought on by undue 'pampering' and self-indulgent decadence, it should be treated instead as evidence of 'decline' (17). Whereas 'strong' pessimism encourages the repudiation of existing values as not merely 'fictitious' but principally a means of 'domination' over or inhibition of 'nature', in the process rejecting their 'system' in the interests of making possible new ways of life, 'weak' pessimism merely succumbs to the 'immense generalization' or 'pathological' inference that life has absolutely no meaning, in order to languish hopelessly in its own decadent state (20). The latter is therefore habitually disillusioned with life, in a way that the former radically is not. Indeed, the self-regarding modernism of the 'weak' and 'gloomy' form is precisely what is to be broken by its 'active' counterpart. But how is this distinction between 'active' and 'passive' pessimism to fare, devoid as it is of the stabilizing presence of a 'true' polar opposite ('optimism')? Since the onset of nihilism is characterized by the passing of values into their opposite (radical devaluation), is it such a simple matter to hold apart alternative forms of pessimism in a cultural environment where everything is increasingly turned into its other?

In contrast to 'weary' or 'exhausted' pessimism of the passive variety, active nihilism is constantly on the attack (24). While, rather than simply contemplating it with complacent languor, active nihilism pursues 'disintegration' with energetic vigour, Nietzsche insists that it has no logical ends or 'goals' as such (25). And yet, in a way that is perhaps fittingly illogical, he writes immediately, 'we have an *aim* which requires us to offer human sacrifices, run any risk and assume the most terrible responsibilities'. Active nihilism aims to be aimless, sets itself the target of annihilating 'human' objectives. It even takes responsibility for its own irresponsibility, while at the same time wishing to 'avoid responsibility', even if through recourse to 'fatalism' (23). If nihilism devastates the question it itself insists upon – 'To what end?' (23) – it simultaneously runs the risk of a secular or devalued reinvention of 'cardinal values' (22), as Nietzsche terms them. He seems well aware of this risk, and is acutely capable of its itemization, producing lists of new 'ends' that spring up in contemporary times, 'ends' that openly acknowledge and yet powerfully repress nihilism's intensifying force. That said, just as much as creating new 'ends' may be 'a sign of *insufficient* strength' (24), disbelief in 'ends' is also what justifies the 'weak-willed and faint-hearted' pessimism so disparaged by Nietzsche. (Elsewhere in the text, Nietzsche bemoans a 'European pessimism' still in its infancy that has not yet discovered a '*motive for conduct*' [28].) In this sense, it proves harder than one might think to decisively demarcate alternative pessimisms, even though their differentiation seems critical. Indeed, it is no less difficult to shelter either type of pessimism from the values they decry; there is even the chance that – even if as an expression of its anarchic illogicality – 'active' nihilism risks greater contamination by existing values. Thus it is telling that Nietzsche writes:

> I have only quite recently admitted to myself that I was the quintessential nihilist all along: the energy and radicalism with which I progressed as a nihilist deceived me about this fundamental fact. When we are making progress towards a goal, it is hard to believe that our fundamental tenet is 'strictly speaking there are no goals'. (25)

Repeating perhaps the paradoxical conditions of self-revelation characterizing Christian salvation, Nietzsche (unlike the immature pessimists of Europe) 'progresses' towards his ownmost nihilism as if towards a pre-ordained goal, in the process hazarding the terrible trinity of 'purpose', 'unity' and 'truth'. Perhaps this very impurity of nihilism in relation to its declared enemies is what saves as much as damns it. But no wonder that nihilism is at once 'the *normal* condition' (24) – indeed, there is no alternative that might allow its specific differentiation (so that for Nietzsche it ultimately becomes a 'loose' and purely symptomatic term [31–32]) – while, at the same time, 'forms of *imperfect* nihilism' everywhere surround and indeed threaten to engulf us (26). To try to 'escape' them (that is, without energetically revaluing values) only 'aggravate[s] the situation', although presumably to *perfect* them would be no less aggravating, given the connotations within the Western tradition of both perfection and perfectability. Once more, nihilism is in a quandary of a similar type to that experienced by a 'prototypical' pessimism (one it cannot henceforth simply surpass or replace), a pessimism that is compelled yet incapable of differentiating itself as such, cast therefore in terms of alternative or derivative forms that continually falter, collapse and implode. This quandary, indeed, seems the beginning and end of nihilism, its eventual destiny as much as its original anarchy, both its high-point and its limit.

In his 'Reflections on Nihilism',[2] occasioned by the publication during the 1950s of a new German edition of Nietzsche's works prepared by Karl Schlechta, Maurice Blanchot dwells on the complex histories of Nietzsche's reception in Germany throughout the decades preceding this particular philosophical event, not least the uses to which Nietzsche's name had been put by the National Socialists. As the essay proceeds, however, Blanchot notes the evident 'self-contradiction' that seems to define the character and 'movement' of Nietzsche's thought. Such a phenomenon, he suggests, is less reducible to processes of systematic clarification, or the normalizing dismissal of shortcomings or, indeed, dialectical reintegration, than it is a matter of irreconcilable affirmations provoking Nietzsche's text into a contested space of reading that demands new practices of reading and interpretation. If Nietzsche's attitude to – and articulation of – nihilism seems to fit this billing, Blanchot's subsequent reinterpretation of Nietzsche's recourse to the theory of eternal return leads him to cite the Nietzschean idea that existence itself is tied to nihilism in its most radical form. This observation seems to change everything. 'Until now we thought nihilism was tied to nothingness', writes Blanchot. 'How ill-considered this was: nihilism is tied to being' (149). The idea that nihilism clears a pathway to nothingness wherein the question of being is overcome or exited is thus countered by Blanchot's assertion of the 'impotence of nothingness, the false brilliance of its victories' (149), given that when we think nothingness we are in fact thinking being at its most extreme yet essential limits. It is in this respect that Nietzschean contradiction manifests the 'very sense of his thought' (144): the other of being is itself, the 'end' of nihilism returns us to the origin, and ultimately nihilism itself offers a 'final and rather grim truth', namely that nihilism is its own 'impossibility' (149).

Blanchot accepts that this insight may seem to have 'the air of a joke', but is nevertheless quick to trace out its worldly significance. Since 'all modern humanism, the work of science and planetary development' is driven by a desire to surpass 'what is' – to transform a present that is, as a consequence, each time of asking, negatively marked – the dominant operation of modern culture is to 'derive power' from precisely this work of negation. If such 'mastery' is therefore tied to the negative in a strong sense, the very 'weakness of the negative' that is revealed in nihilism's self-contradiction (unmasking itself 'in the being that cannot be negated') marks, for Blanchot, the absolute or inherent limit of every project of earthly domination. The self-contradictory thought of nihilism thus leads ultimately to an affirmation rather than any sort of denial or revocation. On what does nihilism therefore turn?

It means what it affirms: that the extreme point of nihilism is precisely there where it reverses itself, that nihilism is this very turning itself, the affirmation that, in passing from the No to the Yes, refutes nihilism, but does nothing other than affirm it, and henceforth extends it to every possible affirmation. (150)

6

MAURICE BLANCHOT

HOPE AND POETRY

In his 'Reflections on Nihilism', then, Blanchot argues that Nietzsche's recourse to the theory of eternal return reconnects existence itself to extreme nihilism. Nihilism, in other words, is ultimately tied to being rather than to nothingness. If the 'planetary development' of science and culture is determined by the desire to transformatively overcome or master 'what is' through its continuous negative marking, then the radical 'weakness of the negative' implied by nihilism's self-contradiction – revealing itself 'in the being that cannot be negated' – resists every operation of earthly domination. From this perspective, nihilism passes from the No to the Yes, as Blanchot puts it, refuting itself by affirming its own impossibility, and – in the process of turning from nothingness towards being – extending itself 'to every possible affirmation'. In another text included in *The Infinite Conversation*,[1] meanwhile, Blanchot notes in similar vein that we 'untiringly construct the world in order that the hidden dissolution, the universal corruption that governs "what is" should be forgotten in favor of a clear and defined coherence of notions and objects, relations and forms' (33). The constitutive affirmation of a profoundly self-contradictory nihilism is, in other words, continually resisted by the orderly construction of 'forms, of notions, and of names' in terms of their stably self-identical 'truth' (34). Such a process, however, grants us only shallow mastery. The effort it entails permits 'hope' in 'an illusory beyond' that is grasped positively in terms of both a 'future without death' and a 'logic without chance' (34); a 'beyond' made possible, however, only by the supposedly positive overcoming of lack or negativity in the present. Since such 'hope' misrecognizes the constitutive and original affirmation that, through Nietzsche, we find in nihilism, it betrays 'the more profound hope that poetry (writing) must teach us to reaffirm' (34). A hope against hope, in other words, reconnecting us to the more original albeit radically non-self-identical conditions of being.

Reflecting on a reading by René Char of Hölderlin's poetry, Blanchot quotes him as saying that 'the poem is the realized love of desire that has remained desire'. The poem realizes what is unrealized, as it were, converting desire into love of (unconverted) desire. Blanchot notes that, from Char's point of view, such paradoxical desire (perhaps as self-contradictory as Nietzschean nihilism) might also be called hope, so that poetry might be its other name. Poetry as hope itself, hope against hope. 'This hope is not just any hope', writes Blanchot. It is, perhaps, hope's only hope, the hope that turns it against itself into itself. But we must be careful what we mean by such hope. It is to be invented in ways that resist the 'weak hope' of an ideal or utopian future that poetry in its essential difference from earthly constructivism confronts and discards. Poetry's non-constructivist inventiveness, rather, affirms that which 'escapes the realm of the possible' (41): as Derrida has also taught us, an invention that is merely 'possible', converting already available materials into already conceivable forms, is not invention truly worthy of the name. Whereas Derrida thereby affirms the necessarily impossible conditions of possibility of invention in its most radical sense (as that which occasions the thought of an absolutely unforeseeable future not limited to the constructivist paradigm operating through a restricted economy of the 'negative' marked as present), Blanchot borrows Yves

Bonnefoy's sense of the 'improbable' to depict the conditions of poetic 'hope', those which pertain otherwise than via the 'horizon of probability' or through the 'approbation' of eventual 'proof' (41). If, for Blanchot, this more profound 'hope' must not hope for a constructable future, but instead reconceive of 'what is' affirmatively rather than just negatively, it cannot take its measure according to how *near* or *far* might be the prospect of what it 'hopes' for. For if poetry must newly and inventively affirm 'what is' each time of asking, nevertheless hope for that which is simply *to hand* is no sort of hope at all. Hope can only be hope when it hopes for 'what is always yet to come, and perhaps will never come' (41). In other words, poetry – *as hope* – must, in this Blanchotian sense, somehow always re-mark the essential self-difference of presence, neither disparaging and forgoing the present in the interests of a conceivable–constructable future, nor affirming 'what is' merely in terms of plenitude, self-sufficiency or self-identity. Beyond relation to the near or far, poetic hope hopes to reconnect to the self-difference of presence (what we might term, here, 'the improbable'): 'Relation recaptured where relation is lost' (41). Hope against hope, hope 'most profound when it withdraws from and deprives itself of all manifest hope', while at the same time *appointing* itself anew, in the here and now, in sharp contrast to the chimerical dreams of 'constructivism'. As Blanchot writes, 'True hope – the unhoped for of all hope – is the affirmation of the improbable'. The 'improbable' that is, and is to come. In this sense, the 'improbable' appears not just as that which may be 'only very slightly probable'. It is, more fundamentally, 'infinitely more than the most probable', albeit improbably so (41).

When, as Blanchot remarks, Simone Weil declares that human life is 'impossible', this should be read not merely to reinforce a sense of life's daily misfortunes or absurdities, since ultimately such a portrayal plays into 'negative determinations' that in fact belong to the 'realm of possibility', as we have already characterized it. Instead, for Blanchot this declaration calls us to recognize 'in impossibility our most human belonging to immediate human life' (47). Desire, he says, is this always 'obscure' and ultimately 'unknown', unformulatable, unsayable relation-without-relation to the 'impossible' (48). Or, in other words, poetry.

7

JACQUES DERRIDA

YES, YES

In 'A Number of Yes',[1] in which Derrida celebrates the work of
Michel de Certeau, the 'yes' to language is examined as that which
precedes all questioning, all discourse and, indeed, every subject.
Every possible utterance – whether affirmative or critical, positive
or negative – cannot but acquiesce to this situation, or in other
words cannot but say 'yes' (in whatever it says) to this pre-given
or, rather, presupposed 'yes' to which one always answers or
responds. This 'first' yes *as* 'first' is nonetheless responsive at its
'origin' – always and already saying *yes* – to the utterance which
whether negative or positive demands its response, one that
cannot help but say 'yes' to it even if in the form of a 'no'. It is as if
the second 'yes', at each time of asking, is what presupposes and
therefore gives us the 'first', which, if it is as much a condition as
the source of the second 'yes', begins to find its possibility – since
this 'dualism' is neither stable nor closed – only in the innumerable
and incalculable 'yesses' disseminated across the general space
of what Derrida in his early texts calls writing in its enlarged sense.
For this reason the 'yes, yes' or, better still, all the 'yesses' inscribed
excessively in this undelimitable scene of the 'yes, yes' cannot
be reduced to the self-same object of a linguistic theory, even if
they nevertheless describe the very conditions of language (and,
indeed, of its 'beyond'). For Derrida, the situation of this 'number
of yes' cannot be grasped ontologically or empirically, neither

purely theoretically nor practically. It is neither, and both, inside and outside language, part of it and occasion of it, prior to and subsequent upon it. No science, phenomenology, or predicative discourse can do the situation justice. Instead, this story – since it must remain a story – of the 'yes' at the limits of philosophical (or other forms of) knowledge is only ever the fable that, before the logos, appears as *almost* originary, the original 'yes' inhabited from the first by the (innumerable) possibility of repetition.

The question of the 'yes, yes' is raised, too, in Derrida's essay, 'Ulysses Gramophone: Hear Say Yes in Joyce',[2] where he countersigns both the Joycean text which offers so many coincidental connections that link Derrida to *Ulysses*, and the phrase of Molly Bloom's – 'yes I said yes I will Yes' – that itself provides a further signature. Here, again, we find ourselves in the midst of an unreckonable 'number of yes', somewhere between the near originary 'first' that nevertheless always supposes or demands its repetition in another, and the proliferal 'yesses' which, as in 'A Number of Yes', countersign the 'first' on the borderlines of memory and invention.

The 'yes' therefore 'engages the "performative" of an originary affirmation' (232) beyond the constraints of any descriptive discourse or metalanguage. It is not ultimately subject to the restrictive borders or demarcating operations required by the production of knowledge, which de Certeau himself links to the presence or procedure of the 'no' (albeit a 'no' which, as Derrida reminds us, can never simply oppose itself to the 'yes' or the 'yes, yes' situation). If in de Certeau such a 'yes' seems to have a Christian flavour, specifically that of Pauline theology, Derrida also underlines its Hebraic connections, so that – neither simply Christian nor Jewish, nor for that matter merely 'divine' or 'Nietzschean', as Derrida puts it – it 'belongs without belonging to the whole that it simultaneously institutes and opens' (236).

It is both in and of language, mediated by it, and nonetheless its 'silent accompanist'. The 'yes' presupposes itself, somewhat maddeningly perhaps; it is always already an answer to itself, or in answer of itself – a groundless affirmation without end, but also an 'absolute volitive', as de Certeau puts it, that therefore goes beyond volition, will, agency, activity, object or goal, constitutively doubling and dividing their conceptual identities. The unconditioned affirmation of the 'yes' or 'yes, yes' makes of the unconditional not a transcendental ideal but an openness to whatever may be (as itself always divided and double): the incalculable, the other, event, promise, future.

Such redoubling affirmation, however, is not necessarily a cause for optimism. For it not only includes the possibility of the negative, indeed the very conditions of its possibility; but also demands attentive response to whatever may come, for good or ill, including the absolute worst that may come (that which might even obliterate the very possibility of response). In a recent interview Giorgio Agamben remarked that 'the concepts pessimism and optimism have nothing to do with thought'.[3] From the perspective of 'A Number of Yes', this assertion has a rather Heideggerian feel to it: in the essay, Derrida remarks on Heidegger's idea of the piety of thinking as connected to a form of questioning that, far from concerning itself foremost with the construction or utilization of formal concepts (whether dualistic or not), is first of all an attentiveness or receptivity to the 'yes' of which he wants to speak. Nonetheless, Derrida might reply to Agamben that terms like optimism and pessimism are part of a philosophical language without which thought – whether despite itself or not – cannot find expression, even if such language at the same time antagonizes thought, reduces thought, damages or divides it from itself. Still, the situation of the 'yes, yes' certainly falls on neither side of the optimism–pessimism opposition in any simple

sense, and for that matter calls into question its pertinence for the
thinking of an originary affirmation made possible by its own rather
maddening deconstructibility: 'yes, yes'. Indeed, perhaps it is this
very situation as something like the impossible-founding scene
of deconstruction that simultaneously occasions accusations of
Derrida's optimism or unreconstructed idealism, on the one hand,
and allegations of his resigned pessimism, nihilism or negativity,
on the other. In anticipation of an 'other' beyond anticipation,
deconstruction may seem – despite rumours to the contrary –
radically optimistic rather than playfully or paralysingly negative.
Nonetheless, strictly speaking deconstruction is to be confused
with neither hope nor despair. Instead, its radical openness to
whatever may come demands hospitality, invention and decision
without the comfort or impediment of given conditions or limits.
For deconstruction, openness to the future is not a matter of
advocating or awaiting better times, it is one of affirming the
split and unstable resources of the present – the 'other' of the
present that everywhere constitutes, supplements and exceeds
it: an always deconstructible 'present' that, however impossibly,
demands response and responsibility. Not once and for all, but
over and over, never quite the same, never quite done, always
too quick and too slow, too soon and too late, never properly
grounded, struggling to keep up, yet always still to come.

For Derrida, the double and divided law of the *demos* –
tied inextricably to both freedom and equality, difference and
sameness, etc. – means that democratic negotiation is effectively
inconcludable. In this sense, 'true' democracy is not achievable
as such, and Derrida is often quick to distinguish his notion of 'the
democracy to come' from the concept of an ideal or utopian state
that could be projected onto the horizon of a constructable future
in which 'democracy' might at last attain absolute self-identity or
self-presence. Divided or *différant* at its very origin, democracy

cannot make itself fully present, or render presence unto itself. Nor should it want or seek to, since the certitude and fixity of a fully established or 'ideal' democratic state would doubtless lessen as much as increase the chances of the democratic experience as an always aporetic one. This aporia of the *demos* – the internecine or auto-immune struggle among its different and divided resources – calls instead for ceaseless vigilance, uncomplacent politics, highly singular engagement and always inventive decision. Since this enduring struggle cannot be resolved by recourse to constructed laws, customs or norms, we find in the democratic 'situation' the very promise of the future. This is why Derrida suggests that it is democracy which in precisely the *here-now* grants the future its possibility – including that of the meaning which democracy may itself yet acquire, for better or worse.

8

EMMANUEL LEVINAS

SOCIALITY AND SOLITUDE

In *Time and the Other*, an early important work appearing in print soon after the end of the Second World War, Levinas asks how existence is taken up by the existent being.[1] In order to distinguish or isolate itself from the impersonal *il y a* – the 'there is' described by Levinas in terms of 'the irremissibility of pure existing' not attributable to anyone or anything as such (47)[2] – the 'existent' must undertake the work of self-identification, thereby enclosing themselves in a unity in which aloneness appears as the constitutive and indeed 'absolutely intransitive' element (42). While the 'consciousness' that arises from the existent's decisive break with the infinite 'vigilance' of anonymous existence therefore rests somewhat paradoxically on 'the power to sleep' as a certain puncturing of its 'irremissibility' (51), nonetheless the advent of this 'consciousness' puts the existent in immediate contact with their existing – Levinas speaks of the 'crispation' or curling and closing up of the self upon itself – in such a way that existence is thereafter borne as an 'attribute' (52). The existence attributed to the existent thus establishes at once its new-found mastery, 'virility' and freedom, and its monadic solitude.

For Levinas, such positing of the existent being is a function of the present as 'a rip' in 'the endless fabric of existing' (52).

However, since by definition this 'present' looks to establish immediate contact with itself, it not only 'rips apart' or tears into, but 'joins together again', joining or returning itself to itself in a way that creates precisely the milieu for the being attributed with existence. Since, essentially, it therefore fulfils a constitutive 'function' rather than being a temporal 'moment' as such, Levinas is quick to underline that this present is not an instant or 'point' within a 'stretch of time' characterized by linear sequence and duration, but instead an 'event' through which 'something comes to start out from itself' (52). In this sense, for Levinas we are not yet in the midst of 'time' properly speaking, far from it. In fact, the 'solitude' of the existent being, cemented in an 'intransitive' present, is described by him as the very 'absence of time' (57).

The existent's unity and solitude also entails its incapacity to detach itself from itself, its pure or 'intransitive' preoccupation with itself constituting a form of self-enchainment or self-encumbrance that Levinas describes in terms of the subject's 'materiality'. The pure freedom of the existent being's starting out from itself is thus tempered by an absolute responsibility for itself. In this perspective, materiality is not – as philosophers had long held – an expression of the 'contingent fall of the spirit into the tomb or prison of a body' (56). It is rather the inaugurating heaviness of an existent being riveted to itself as the everyday consequence or 'matter' of its own manner of existing. It is, in fact, 'the upsurge of the subject in its existent freedom' (56).

If the solitude accomplished by the subject bogs it down (63), then attempts at self-separation in order to encourage 'forgetfulness' of the existent's plight should be enumerated and assessed. Levinas identifies 'light' and 'reason' – enjoyment or knowledge of the objects that one encounters in the world – as pathways to such forgetfulness. However, to 'illuminate' is to experience the object as if it was *for me* or was somehow 'mine'. Thus, 'light' does not estrange the captive self but instead re-inscribes the 'outside' within the realm of the subject's solitude or self-knowledge. Likewise, 'reason' constrains and rearticulates externality on its own terms as much as it promotes objectivity. Instead, Levinas argues, existent life might break with the monadic predicament in which it is mired from the outset only if it truly 'encounters an event that stops its everyday transcendence from falling back upon a point that is always the same' (66).

For Levinas, suffering is the very condition of the existent being in the sense that there is 'an absence of all refuge' (69) in its unremitting exposure to its own attributes. Suffering is not just compounded but in fact described by the subject's inability to detach from its own suffering. First and foremost, the existent suffers itself. However, Levinas argues that suffering itself betokens 'the proximity of death' (69). In suffering there is the feeling that death is its 'end'. The constitutive intensity and prolongation of suffering therefore meets with 'an unknown that is impossible to translate in terms of light' (69), indeed an absolute 'unknowability' which in turn harbours the (im)possible 'event' that for Levinas would mark the limit of the subject's accomplishments: self-identification, presence, freedom, mastery, and so forth. For Levinas, far from constituting the ownmost possibility of the existent being, death could never be an attribute of the subject. Death is absolutely other, totally unassimilable, completely alienating, a pure mystery: 'My solitude is thus not confirmed by death but broken by it' (74). And yet because death is unavoidably suffered in life (albeit that the human being is never able to die since death is not an 'ability' of his), death *pluralizes* existence. 'A plurality insinuates itself into the very existing of the existent', writes Levinas (75). No-one is able to die, yet each being that exists through solitude suffers death in this way, taking 'its place on a ground where the relationship with the other becomes possible' (76). For Levinas, this (as it were) impossible possibility of a pluralizing relationship – wholly beyond our own attributes but still endemic for us – finds its 'prototype' in the 'erotic', and is destined to encounter an entirely unencounterable 'future' in the absolutely surprising event heralded by death. If death would seem to threaten total oblivion or obliteration of the being attributed with existence, nonetheless it is in the face of death that we exist. That is to say, we exist in the face of the Other:

> The relationship with the Other, the face-to-face with the Other, the encounter with a face that at once gives and conceals the Other, is the situation in which an event happens to a subject who does not assume it, who is utterly unable in its regard, but where nonetheless in a certain way it is in front of the subject. (78–79)

Time properly speaking is for Levinas the abyssal exposure of the otherwise atemporal or solitudinous present in the face of the future's absolute alterity. Such an exposure could not be reduced to any of the usual temporal motifs of continuity, sequentiality, chronology, dynamism or duration (as if the present were to be suitably rearticulated within a functional temporal schema that contextualized it more widely as some sort of 'point' or 'instant'). An im-possible confrontation of the present with death as the basis of time itself suggests that the 'situation of the face-to-face' suffered by the existent is, in fact, nothing less than 'the very accomplishment of time' (79). As Levinas puts it, the upshot of understanding time from the perspective of alterity is that 'one never again meets with time as a "moving image of eternity"', or in other words Platonic time. 'The future is not buried in the bowels of a preexistent eternity … It is absolutely other and new' (80). Time properly speaking means that the present finds no equivalence in the future.

Surveying a philosophical landscape characterized by
varieties of existentialism, phenomenology and Marxism,
Levinas alludes to the seemingly 'insurmountable antagonism'
within contemporary thought between 'the hope for a better
society and the despair of solitude', whereby one perspective
takes the arguments of the contrary position not as a point of
debate, engagement or self-reflection, but as a self-evident
reason to deprecate or disqualify the other point of view. Thus,
the 'optimistic constructivism of sociology and socialism' finds
no room for 'the feeling of solitude' that nevertheless haunts its
own epoch. For such 'optimists', as Levinas well understands,
the anxiety of solitude encourages an 'ostrichlike position' that
is at best distractingly irrelevant (mere 'idle chatter') and at worst
mystificatory, and thus ideologically regressive, in terms of a
political need for solidarity, collective works, lucid communication
and social transformation (58–61). In the opening section of Part
II of *Time and the Other*, where these themes re-emerge, Levinas
offers some criticisms and objections concerning the essential
grounds of this antagonism, renewing in the process his earlier
invitation to rethink the 'dialectic' that it indicates. Going back
to the opening pages of the text, where such themes are first
announced, we better grasp the deeper argument of this work:
namely because pluralization is accomplished in the face of the
other and not by means of a commonality established through the
side-by-side relation, Levinas cannot but reject the exclusionary
and oppositional definition of 'solitude by sociality and of sociality
by solitude' (40). For him, pluralization is accomplished thanks to
the solitude suffered by the existent. It is possible because of, and
not despite, the 'intransitive' element of aloneness through which
existence is assumed by the living being. Far from arising beyond,
against or outside of solitudinous existence, the very possibility of
'sociality' is in fact inscribed *within* it – albeit a 'sociality' riven with

the alterity which splits or opens the subject's identity in its abyssal relation to time, death and the other.

Given his allusion to the 'optimistic' outlook that characterizes forms of thought oriented towards 'sociality', Levinas's critical reconsideration of the mutually self-reinforcing distinction between 'sociality' and 'solitude' within modern debates also implies an unpicking of the long-standing partition dividing 'optimism' from 'pessimism' within philosophy. It is noteworthy that he is careful not to resort to the description of those philosophies leaning more towards 'solitude' as pessimistic. Given Levinas's overt recourse to the 'optimistic' label where socially oriented perspectives are concerned (sounding not a little like a slur), for some readers this doubtless exposes his deeper intellectual sympathies. However, the absence of the word also suggests that the 'pessimistic' mantle which normally accompanies accounts of any philosophy of 'solitude' is being discarded by Levinas for more essential reasons. If 'solitude' is the basis for pluralization where human existence is concerned, then 'pessimism' seems the wrong term all of a sudden, if by that very same term 'solitude' is returned inertly to itself as a matter of routine. That being said, one still suspects that the 'optimism-pessimism' divide falters in *Time and the Other* largely because Levinas, by opening up a new perspective within the thought of 'solitude', is able to redefine philosophical 'pessimism' itself (in the process, perhaps, dispensing with its very name). Rather like the suffering existent, it is this branch or 'side' of philosophy that is made to suffer the 'work' of alterity, as it were. Optimism gives ground, in other words, as the very ground of 'transformation'[3] (61).

As is well known, many commentators on Levinas observe in his philosophy an optimistic affirmation of radical exposure to the other on the part of the subject, this being the very source of ethical possibility; but several also find such optimism's limit in a more pessimistic viewpoint where the prospect of full-scale transfer into the social or political world is concerned.[4] If Levinas was, on more than one occasion, quick to dismiss the validity or usefulness of a distinction between optimism and pessimism, famously objecting to the portrayal of his work as advancing an 'optimistic morality',[5] it is nevertheless interesting that in *Time and the Other*, far from it being the case that social or political pessimism simply curtails human optimism on a 'moral' plane, we discover that the ostensibly pessimistic wing of philosophy may provide the means to pluralize possibility, opening up solitude to an alterity that just cannot be re-accommodated within the self.

9

SIGMUND FREUD

'A TIME-CONSUMING BUSINESS'

In what James Strachey describes as one of Freud's final 'strictly psycho-analytic writings' published during his lifetime, appearing almost twenty years after his last 'purely technical work', Freud in 'Analysis Terminable and Interminable' reflects on the various obstacles confronting a successful analysis.[1] Here, he considers not only the barriers which occur in particular circumstances as an individual analysis proceeds, but the more persistent obstacles faced by psychoanalysis now that it has reached a certain level of maturity as an established practice over several decades. Thus, Freud's essay proceeds on the basis of a sustained analogy between the lasting impact of psychoanalytic treatment on individual patients and the question of psychoanalysis's durability itself.

Freud begins by observing that psychoanalytic therapy if conducted rigorously is 'a time-consuming business' (216). If analysis had developed and indeed matured on the strength of its initial resistance to the impatience of medical science with the extended treatment of mental illnesses, nevertheless as time went by certain practitioners sought to innovate with psychoanalytic methods in order to shorten the duration of analysis. Otto Rank's attempt to pinpoint primal trauma as the key to fast-tracking psychic health is singled out for note by Freud. Presumably the benefits of a more truncated approach would not be lost on prospective patients or their families; and more widely the optimism displayed by Rank concerning his own supposed breakthrough fitted perfectly, we are told, with the climate of hope and prosperity found in 1920s America, presented by Freud as in stark contrast to the seemingly never-ending 'post-war misery of Europe'. Rank's method was therefore 'a child of its time', 'designed to adapt the tempo of analytic therapy to the haste of American life' (216). A fresh outlook and a quick fix for ready money: optimism, novelty, wealth and speed here constituted a striking historic ensemble. For Freud, however, Rank's brainchild was laughably premature, and destined to be short-lived. He likens its methodology to the cartoonishly comic scenario of a fire-brigade tackling a blazing house-fire by removing the overturned oil-lamp that caused it. Far from simply expediting the fire-fighting, such action just hastens the total destruction of the burning home. 'No doubt a considerable shortening of the brigade's activities would be effected by this means', Freud drily quips (217). Time is the only thing that is saved. If Rank's gimmicky technique disappeared just as quickly as it was concocted, in the process the confident clustering together of prosperity, novelty, optimism and acceleration proved far from durable, Freud suggests: 'The theory and practice of Rank's experiment are now things of the past – no less than American "prosperity" itself' (217).

However, Freud takes this recollection as a cue to reflect on his own efforts to speed up analytic treatment. Needless to say, he undertook such experiments way ahead of Rank! Investigating quick-win solutions in the setting of pre-war Europe, years before the false and rather forced optimism of the American 1920s, Freud tells us he was rapidly able to dismiss the potential short-term benefits of such an expedited approach. Just before hostilities broke out, Freud had chosen to address the disappointing results of treatment in the case of one of his patients by fixing an artificial and impending deadline for its termination. The patient in question, a wealthy Russian (tellingly enough) whose more fundamental progress was impeded by a level of complacency brought on by the partial success of his early analysis, was made to confront his deeper problems with greater haste by means of withdrawing the reassurance of unlimited treatment. At the time, the results were misleadingly promising: 'When he left me in the midsummer of 1914, with as little suspicion as the rest of us what lay so shortly ahead, I believed that his cure was radical and permanent' (217). Here, if wealth (admittedly of time as much as of money) presented itself as an obstacle to analytic optimism, rather than its aid, nevertheless a hurried approach once more produced only ironic outcomes. Like an all-consuming house-fire, the unforeseen effects of a devastating world war quickly reversed the short-term gains of the abruptly ended analysis, as Freud himself readily acknowledges: 'I have already reported that I was mistaken', he writes (218). Sure enough, the symptoms returned, although it is a little unclear whether the new-found poverty and humility of the patient's post-war existence actually mitigated rather than aggravated the recurrence of mental illness in this once-imperious Russian lately fallen from grace. Freud is quick-witted in his grasp of 'fast' analysis as long-term folly, and not slow to put the breaks on the dizzying combination of wealth, optimism and speed that fed Rank's novel approach.

Freud assesses the risks of an early termination of analysis in a twofold way. An artificially imposed end-point may potentially work only if the timing is right. And one doesn't get second chances: 'The saying that a lion only springs once must apply here' (219). The fixing of an end must constitute neither an empty threat nor a false promise. The trouble is, as Freud's examples have already shown, one can never truly know whether the time is right. This is not just because it is difficult to establish if progress is sufficient to conclude treatment. Freud recognizes that, in any analysis, aspects of the patient's 'childhood history' may be slow in coming to light, indeed may powerfully resist analysis and so remain hidden as a consequence of therapy, *because of* treatment and not despite it. From this point of view, seeming improvement may well conceal the deeper preservation of fundamental obstacles to analytic success. Termination on the strength of an assessment of progress is therefore as likely to be spectacularly ill-considered as it may be expertly well informed. The end of analysis might just as much herald the triumph of a prevailing sickness, as offer consoling proof of its correction. Once the question of a fitting 'time' for analysis is shattered by the seemingly inescapable risk of duplicitous endings, all optimism appears devastated.

Thus Freud moves on from the issue of analysis's duration to the very question of its possible end. He does so, in a double sense. The issue is not only when, how or whether analysis should it stop, but what is its actual purpose, what can it really achieve? If what doesn't kill you makes you stronger, insofar as the hidden materials stubbornly resistant to therapy are concerned, then analysis only stores up problems for the future. It perhaps even *creates* the future as a problem. Given the advent of what Levinas once called the 'optimistic constructivism of sociology and socialism' as part of the same historic arc that saw the birth of psychoanalysis, a 'constructivism' responsible for the modern construction of the future as a concept or category, this looks like a rather weird infecting of optimism with pessimism on psychoanalysis's part. The very possibility of the future, in other words, is this radical doubling of optimism with its other. Yet perhaps because it is so 'doubled' with doubt in order that the future itself may be possible, optimism might withstand its own seeming devastation, at least in some respects.

From the second part of the essay onwards, Freud considers the deep and perhaps relentless struggle between, on the one hand, congenital or constitutional factors causing traumatic conditions for the analysand, and, on the other, the power of the ego strengthened by psychoanalysis to defend itself against their continual onslaught. Here, even if analysis initially produces positive results, later on in life illness can recur, prompting the question of whether this recurrence is due to inadequate or incomplete treatment of the original ailment – a process which if better conducted might have prevented future problems altogether, but which if deficient renders them somewhat inevitable – or whether the apparent relapse may spring from a wholly new conflict or trauma that could not have been foreseen, but that, once occurring, inevitably retriggers suffering – a viewpoint which supposes that analysis will only ever be capable of relieving rather than removing constitutional defects. Since, as we have already seen, it is ultimately impossible to know whether progress is really sufficient to justify ending analysis, and since the advent of a new trauma is – at least in Freud's view in 1937 – more contingent than inevitable (and may very well never occur), psychoanalysis need not remonstrate with itself if a fresh outbreak happens. (From this perspective, regardless of the chance of future misfortunes, it is perfectly possible that analysis once concluded can believe itself brought to a fitting end, albeit an 'end' that may itself come to an end at some later date.) Here, one detects a rather odd interaction between a certain type of cheeriness on Freud's part, whereby psychoanalysis is somewhat relieved of responsibility for future illnesses, and the deeper pessimism from which it stems concerning psychoanalysis's fundamental capacity to cure.

In addition to this, Freud also takes a moment to imagine the lively debate between the 'sceptic' who draws from this state of affairs the pessimistic conclusion that, regardless of its limited or provisional achievements, psychoanalysis is ultimately bound to fail one way or another, and the 'optimist' or 'ambitious' person who believes that the development of psychoanalytic thought and practice is itself not yet concluded or even anywhere near a fully mature end. Since many of the relevant case studies which might be reviewed at the time of the essay's composition belong to the period of psychoanalysis's infancy, it may be hoped in time – even if much later on – that a more positive assessment of psychoanalytic outcomes might be possible. Here, once more, the developmental advances in analytic technique mirror the situation of the individual for whom the duration of analysis is a key question: while in retrospect a degree of pessimism seems readily justified concerning the treatment's 'ending' or its satisfactory resolution, equally it is always too soon to tell whether more can be hoped from the future, precisely since one shouldn't be too quick to pronounce endings of any kind. Yet again, pessimism and optimism seem much less clearly distinct or neatly opposed than complexly embroiled in one another, conditioning and contributing to the prospects of the other even while establishing certain resistant limits that determine their interaction. In other words, 'it ain't over 'til it's over' is both the cry of hope and despair of 'Analysis Terminable and Interminable'.

Notwithstanding the above, the prophylactic capacity of psychoanalysis to protect by inoculating its patients against subsequent relapse remains a question that Freud finds himself unable to quickly dismiss. Even if one cannot permanently remove certain constitutional factors, would it be possible through the workings of the initial analysis to insure against certain types of recurrence? Here is the problem. Since psychoanalysis aims to positively adjust the ego by strengthening its defences and hence its capacity to tame instinctual forces, the risk is that, in order to oppose such suppression, those very same instincts will need to toughen up, step up to the plate, call in reinforcements, bring their 'A' game. Psychoanalysis therefore provokes not merely a battle of strength but an arms race in which the ever-intensifying use of deterrence leads to the brink of the nuclear destruction it aims to prevent.[2] The question of psychoanalysis's 'ends' here acquires a new-found ironic resonance. Even – and perhaps especially – if both psychoanalysis and its 'constitutional' enemies grow stronger as time passes, the idea of analysis as some kind of deterrent is as much a cause for gloom as optimism, even if Freud places considerable faith in the brinkmanship of a brokered peace. 'These new dams are of a quite different degree of firmness from the earlier ones; we may be confident that they will not give way so easily before a rising flood of instinctual strength' (227), he protests. But this sounds too much like a political rather than a scientific pronouncement, and it is certainly somewhat at odds with the more pessimistic remarks Freud makes just a few pages later, about the near-irresistible power of the 'big battalions' (240) of hidden instinctual life. Yet Freud confesses himself unable to 'give up' or bring to an end this 'theory', such dreadful store does he set by it, even if analytic experience 'is not yet wide enough for us to come to a settled conclusion' (228). Once again it is difficult to tell whether such critical inexperience might lead to disastrous miscalculation on the part of an immature science, or whether the future may itself be redeemed once we are able to move beyond the terrible brinkmanship of the present. Is the end of mere 'hope' to be wished for here, as much as its fragile persistence?

Freud confesses himself deeply divided over the question of the power of psychoanalysis. Is it the decisive factor in holding the worst at bay, or – given the equally complicated and compromised everyday lives of unanalysed people – would it make much odds, indeed might it even be better, if psychoanalysis had never existed? Does analysis make the real difference? 'I really cannot commit myself to a decision on this point, nor do I know whether a decision is possible at this time', writes Freud (228). With this inner crisis of confidence or constitutive anxiety characteristic of every (nuclear) power, Freud feels tempted to subscribe to the malicious dictum: 'Every step forward is only half as big as it looks at first' (228). Just as in pre-war Europe of the early twentieth century, Freud traces the conditions of optimism's end(s) – in at least a double sense – in 1937 his remarks on prophylactic protection or deterrence anticipate a nuclear paradigm he can yet barely countenance.

At the same time, however, another image of modern warfare suggests itself when during the fourth section of his essay Freud considers the idea that, in order to prevent 'future conflicts' that may indeed wheel out of all control, present ones might be deliberately stirred up. The intentional production and conscious management of a crisis designed to counteract subsequent events (whether they are predictable or not) surely reminds the contemporary reader of certain twenty-first-century conflicts, for example those in the Middle East, not least since to fully minimize the risks it sought to address the limits of such planned aggression would be difficult to determine. Following Freud's train of thought throughout 'Analysis Terminable and Interminable', it would seem logical to suppose that to desist in stirring up trouble might open the door to unknown horrors on a grander scale. It would be hard to know where or when to stop. Not wishing to advance further with this line of thought, once more Freud takes a step backwards, recoiling from the implications of his own thinking. Indeed, the very idea is unthinkable:

> Nobody thinks of purposely conjuring up new situations of suffering in order to make it possible for the latent instinctual conflict to be treated. This would not be much to boast as a prophylactic achievement. (232)

Freud therefore establishes the rule that the 'productive measure must not produce the same situation of danger as is produced in the illness itself' (232). Instead, the only methods that prove acceptable in pursuing this form of crisis management are 'the artificial production of new conflicts in the transference (conflicts which after all, lack the character of reality)' and 'the arousing of such conflicts in the patient's imagination' (232–33). Yet the deliberate provocation of so-called artificial conflict, supplemented by the intentionally motivated internalization of conflict in the other (reinforced by overt suggestion), recalls precisely those techniques of war we witness on a daily basis today. From this perspective, one might equally view Freud's stepping back as merely a way to facilitate next steps, shall we say. Unsurprisingly, Freud is troubled by his own suggestion, and tries once more to back away from its consequences. Nevertheless, he still advocates that the analyst 'tell the patient about the possibilities of other instinctual conflicts' and 'arouse his expectation that such conflicts may occur' in the hope that 'such information and this warning may have the effect of activating in him one of the conflicts we have indicated, in a modest degree and yet sufficiently for treatment' (233). This sounds very much like the West's strategy where terrorism is concerned. While Freud himself declares that such techniques are limited in their effectiveness to the extent that in the majority of cases they fall upon deaf ears, we know today that this is expectation is, of course, intrinsic to the so-called war on terror waged on an entire region (depending as it does on a certain degree of widespread passivity as much as actively violent opposition).

Inhabiting the psychic space of a politics of international conflict yet to come, with increasing pessimism Freud concludes that the enemy is undefeatable, that its congenital or constitutional disposition makes conflict ultimately insoluble, and that resistance is as much created as it is combatted through the types of engagement fostered within the confrontational situation of analysis. Since operations – however tactical they may be – will always strike a hostile bedrock incapable of permanent resolution, even peace-keeping enjoys limited effectiveness and is probably doomed to failure. The enemy lacks 'the capacity for change and further development' (241); it vacillates fearfully between 'inertia', 'entropy' and absolutely destructive 'aggression' (242–43). If by this point Freud appears to suffer debilitating despair in the face of an unconquerable adversary, it is not long before he groups psychoanalysis with 'education and government' as similarly 'impossible' professions (248), once more recalling certain prevalent attitudes to the Middle East today. But the problem is compounded since, like every politician, each analyst also has their own battles to fight on the domestic front. As susceptible as any other individual to the hostile forces buried within the self, for practical reasons trainees benefit from merely a 'short and incomplete' (248) period of analysis themselves (albeit the definition of full and finished therapy is hardly readily forthcoming in this text). While such treatment encourages the trainee to become analytically self-reflective, in the interests of his patients as much as himself, nevertheless Freud observes that many therapists 'make use of defensive mechanisms which allow them to divert the implications and demands of analysis from themselves' (249), projecting their own deficiencies onto others and in the process displacing and concealing justified criticisms they might otherwise face themselves. In this context, Freud reminds us of the well-known adage that 'when a man is endowed with power it is hard for him not to misuse it' (249), recalling once more the motif of warfare that Freud himself evokes throughout the essay, and adding a further layer of analysis to the interpretation of hostilities past and present.

While analysis like war must sometimes be brought to a close for practical reasons, it is 'not easy to foresee a natural end, even if one avoids any exaggerated expectations and sets the analysis no excessive tasks' (250). By 1937, even the most modest therapeutic ambitions invite a degree of pessimism on Freud's part. Nevertheless, since the future itself – of psychoanalysis, as much as of the patient – depends on this seemingly unpromising state of affairs, a strange optimism perhaps resurfaces. If, in at least a double sense, the 'end' of psychoanalysis is not yet in sight, *and might never be*, then the death-instinct that so stubbornly resists and even contaminates analysis may never have the final word.[3] Notwithstanding this, what it might mean to suffer such 'non-ending' is no less fearful – for all concerned. It is not merely 'a time-consuming business'.

10

MELANIE KLEIN

'THERAPEUTIC PESSIMISM' IN KRISTEVA'S VIEW

In her critical biography of psychoanalyst Melanie Klein,[1] Julia Kristeva contrasts the central role played by desire in the formation of the Freudian unconscious with the Kleinian emphasis on anxiety as of pivotal importance in psychic life. What might seem to be at stake in Klein's reworking of Freudian psychoanalysis is therefore a rebalancing or even restructuration of the relationship between Eros and Thanatos. For Kristeva, the frustration experienced by the Kleinian ego in search of gratification is not the source of a 'lack' that re-stimulates desire so much as it is the motor of anxious feelings that are, indeed, 'automated' prior to the separation which also marks transition from the paranoid-schizoid to the depressive state. Frustration, in other words, precedes the integration of the ego such that it facilitates object-formation rather than simply re-inscribing 'lack' as a sort of desiring-tolerance.

Kristeva seeks to demonstrate that, for Klein, the unconscious is constituted by a *fear* as much as a *desire* for life. Fear for life has, of course, at least double meaning. One may fear for one's life in the sense of fearfulness of death. But fear for life also implies being scared for the duration of life, as if life itself is constituted by fear (fear for itself). While the death drive is, thereby, as Kristeva herself puts it, 'dialectically restored to its positive version, which is the very preservation of life' (83), at the same time fear of life is for 'the sake of life' (83), in life's interests and perhaps at its very origins. If Klein regarded Freud as rather neglectful in properly considering such fearfulness, for Kristeva her reinterpretation of psychoanalysis therefore intimately reconnects the life and death drive through the specific workings of anxiety – without which, indeed, one would risk psychosis as the end-result of entirely unfrustrated desires (a process arrested by the onset of phobia as a response to lapses in paternal authority and prohibition).

Kristeva compares Klein's thought to that of Hannah Arendt in the sense that, despite their obvious differences, a proper concern for life emerges through regard for that which threatens it. Arendt's concern for natality as constitutive of our capacity for life is therefore contrasted with Klein's 'therapeutic relentlessness' in tracking the human paroxysms which occur at the frontiers of life and death, love and hatred, anxiety and desire. The 'capturing' (85) or constitution of the object that happens as desire is converted into anxiety allows for a recasting of psychoanalysis wherein the products of the unconscious consist in thought as much as pleasure, albeit thought constitutively distorted through inhibition, anxiety or other forms of psychic defence. Sadistic drives, aggressive impulses and cruel actions all stem from this fear for life at the heart of life, and they seem irreducible at a certain point. In several of Klein's case studies, as Kristeva points out, life's own concern – its self-concern – manifests itself in terms of a wish or fantasy on the part of the living to eat the living, whereby such cannibalistic ingestion of life by itself reflects the recasting of desire as anxiety. 'Unconscious sadism' therefore splits life's objects, whether they are considered 'internal' or 'external'. But 'good' and 'bad' are not merely differentiated; instead, the splitting of 'reality' for the human being confronts unconscious drives with what Kristeva describes as a deforming representation which blocks Freudian access to gratification, whether real or imagined. It is as if destructiveness is not so much the means by which desire ultimately realizes itself, overcoming impediments to its own goals, but is instead desire's self-realization – and non-realization – as such. Yet, of course, right from the beginning violence also 'reins in', deals with or addresses anxiety (88). Since this aspect of a constitutive 'splitting' affects every 'fantasy', every 'object' of psychic life, the psychic defences of the ego (for instance, those facilitated by the image of the 'good breast') are as much damaged as they are maintained by the impetus received from the death drive. With Klein's work, we are therefore in the midst of the 'constant work of the negative and an interminable sublimation of mourning, with the death drive sustaining psychic development' (88) in such a way that Freudian 'hallucinatory wish-fulfilment' (characterized by Kristeva as a 'plenitude of bliss') is always threatened and undermined by an absolutely constitutive negativity. Since, for Klein, the 'intensity' of the 'destructive drive' is 'innate', it is arguable whether Kleinianism ultimately succumbs to 'therapeutic pessimism'. What might Kleinian analysis actually *do* with the 'constitutional basis' of psychic life that it claims to uncover? How, on this basis, could the analytic subject be treated? Is the answer to fully recognize (and thereby, perhaps, take through to its very end) the life–death relation – in which case, what might be the consequences? Or should analysis instead seek interventions designed to transform that same relation – in which case: to what ends? The fact that Kristeva can find no ready solution to these questions in the Kleinian text leads her to discern a 'generalized pessimism' in Klein's work concerning the 'relevance' of analytic treatment itself. Even while the latter 'concedes its limitations', the deep quandaries presented to us by

Klein's vision of psychic development and psychic life suggest that, even in limited form, therapy may ultimately prove inconsequential. A 'good environment' may do little to 'modify the constitutional basis' (89), especially given the seemingly relentless operations of splitting and conversion undertaken through the work of a constitutive negativity. While, as Kristeva notes, 'a deficient environment or extensive deprivation' may well 'aggravate innate aggressive qualities', she herself has already conceded that Klein provides scant answer to the question of whether what is innate should be 'optimally realized' rather than actively transformed through 'transference, interpretation, and a new environment'. While Kristeva concludes that the psychoanalyst should bravely continue the task of reducing splitting and aiding the ego in 'integrating split-off parts' (89), this recommendation suffers from the assumption which Kristeva has already called into question, namely that efforts to derive therapeutic benefits from the hoped-for transformation of a 'constitutional' state of affairs are to be postulated as essentially worthwhile from the perspective of Klein's 'therapeutic pessimism'. On the terms of Kristeva's own discussion of Klein's reinterpretation of psychoanalysis, this seems little more than conjecture. Whether resting on a case of unfounded optimism, false hope, or rather anxious desire, the assistance offered by analysis in the working-through to a depressive state characterized by at least partial re-integration must not only affirm as much as confront constitutive anxiety, but – whether it seems beneficial or not – must of necessity leave unanswered the essential dilemma posed by Kleinian pessimism: Can we ever be sure that therapy is, on balance, advantageous? From this point of view, however, psychoanalysis might – indeed, must – be ventured in only the most radical sense of the term.

11

JULIA KRISTEVA

'PSYCHOANALYSIS – A COUNTERDEPRESSANT'

Julia Kristeva's *Black Sun*[1] – as its subtitle suggests, a sustained reflection on depression and melancholia – opens with a text that seems to announce psychoanalysis as a 'counterdepressant'; although of course the chapter's heading, 'Psychoanalysis – A Counterdepressant', whether deliberately or not, also hints at the possibility that psychoanalysis itself may be in some need of countering (perhaps by Kristeva's own text) where depression is concerned. While the distinction drawn by Kristeva in this essay between psychoanalytic practice and the administering of antidepressants seems, on the face of it, an obvious one, nevertheless it is less clear in what sense psychoanalysis might be – if, indeed, it is taken to be – a 'counterdepressant'. Psychiatrists, we are told, treat melancholia as an irreversible illness that is responsive only to antidepressants (Kristeva in fact calls the field of study which examines their effects 'promising' if currently 'imprecise'), presumably implying that psychoanalysis offers a different reaction or approach that may 'counter' depression without merely reducing, regulating or blocking it through the introduction of an anti- or foreign body or a chemical supplement into the system. (Unless, of course, psychoanalysis itself depresses, and is therefore in want or need of countering.)

But perhaps tellingly it is never made explicit by Kristeva how, if at all, psychoanalytic practice may constitute such an alternative to antidepressants or how, in other words, psychoanalysis may counteract despair.

Perhaps in the context of a certain therapeutic pessimism of her own, Kristeva begins by observing that the discourse of melancholy (whether critical, speculative etc.) only acquires meaning if it is written from within the space of melancholia itself, that is by the melancholic. Since Kristeva's writing, not least in this chapter, is obviously deeply permeated by psychoanalytic thought, it surely follows that psychoanalysis must be melancholic to have anything to say about melancholia. But how, if at all, does such psychoanalysis serve as a 'counterdepressant'? Are we to take the hint, and assume that psychoanalysis must be depressed in some way, or somehow capable of depression, so as to counter depression itself? In order to 'counter', one might think that you'd first of all need to identify, locate or situate depression *as such*, and yet this is less than easily done. Kristeva writes that her 'pain' is 'the hidden side of her philosophy' (4), somehow inaccessible to it, and yet presumably a core element and critical part, like the black sun of Kristeva's title that dazzles and blinds through the sheer amplitude of light it conveys. 'The depressed person is a philosopher', writes Kristeva, suggesting that since the time of Aristotle philosophy has been the melancholic expression of the anxiety of being, an exceptional 'surfeit' of being's very nature. Philosophy has as its other 'side', if rather buried and mysterious, the 'pain' that constitutes its very possibility.

Depression, meanwhile, involves a radical disenchantment, a deprivation so severe that one hardly knows what may have been lost, including oneself, to the point that the depressed person lacks not merely the lost 'object' but credence or belief itself (thus, they are unable to know how to compensate), becoming in turn

a 'radical, sullen atheist' as Kristeva puts it (5). Depression is not
merely the 'hidden side' of philosophical thought but it is also –
and perhaps not unrelatedly – 'the hidden face of Narcissus',
that which converts the 'mirage' of self-image into a 'shadow of
despair', turning self-reflection into a harbinger of death, without
the subject's even knowing it. The nature or import of despair is no
less elusive than depression itself, since while its meaning is either
simply 'obvious' or else inevitably 'metaphysical', nonetheless for
Kristeva the very possibility of meaning itself derives from despair
as precisely a condition of separation, albeit one that cannot seem
to access its own condition.

Classically, for psychoanalysis (from Freud and Abraham to
Klein) depression involves an aggressivity towards the (lacking
or lost) other as its own origin. Suicidal despair is therefore
aimed, albeit in distorted or veiled ways, at this intolerable other
that one loves–hates and wishes (within oneself) to recuperate–
destroy. To kill in order to cannibalize, and vice versa. And yet,
Kristeva observes, 'the treatment of narcissistic individuals has
led modern analysis to understand another form of depression',
one constituted less by the 'other' as divided object than it is
caused by a 'primitive' sadness brought on by basic emptiness,
fundamental incompleteness:

> Their sorrow doesn't conceal the guilt or the sin felt because of
> having secretly plotted revenge on the ambivalent object. Their
> sadness would be rather the most archaic expression of an
> unsymbolizable, unnameable narcissistic wound, so precocious
> that no outside agent ... can be used as referent. (12)

In this type of depression, 'sadness is really the sole object',
although actually such 'sadness' is more precisely a substitute
object or a *faux* stand-in for the object itself; a non-object

masquerading in its place, even before its place is taken or staked. If in order to 'counter' despair (or depression, or melancholy) we had hoped to identify it as an 'object' of analysis, here we are confronted instead with a profound sadness without object other than itself as non-objectifiable. Kristeva writes, therefore, that in this type of deep depression what is mourned is not the 'Object' as such, but instead the (Kantian) 'Thing' as 'the real that does not lend itself to signification' (13). Following Nerval, the 'Thing' is construed as 'an insistence without presence, a light without representation … an imagined sun, bright and black at the same time' (13). No object, erotic or otherwise, can compensate in this situation, since it is a matter of basic emptiness – 'alone with the unnamed Thing' – as much as of identifiable loss. Destined to remain 'mute and steadfast devotees of their own inexpressible container' (14), imprisoned *with* as much as *by* the 'Thing' that is without or beyond memory, the anguish of narcissists engulfed by their own sadness is 'unspeakable', and so presumably unreceptive to any discourse of despair, depression or the like.

For Kristeva, then, the depressive position that for Klein offers the possibility of reintegration as a means to address schizoid splitting or fragmentation in earlier infancy may be expressed as a reconstitution of such 'sadness' as much as some kind of progression or development away from 'crisis'. Depression, for sure, dispenses with 'the schizoid anguish of fragmentation', but it defends against the angst of (erotic) object-dynamics and not death or despair (emptiness) itself:

> Depressed persons do not defend themselves against death but against the anguish prompted by the erotic object. Depressive persons cannot endure Eros, they prefer to be with the Thing up to the limit of negative narcissism leading them to Thanatos.

They are defended against Eros by sorrow but without defense against Thanatos because they are wholeheartedly tied to the Thing. (20)

How – if at all – does one therefore counteract despair, if it is not obviously treatable (along the lines of an antidepressant treatment), nor even identifiable, objectifiable and thereby readily amenable to speech or (analytic) language as such – as is the case with the particular form of 'sadness' experienced by the depressive narcissist? How does one tackle a depression that may be deeply death-bound as much as it offers defence against disintegration? What should psychoanalysts do, how might they act, in these circumstances? Kristeva indeed writes that psychoanalysts, rather than providing 'neutralizing antidepressants' which is the dubious task of psychiatrists, should act as 'lucid counterdepressants' (24). Here, she suggests that – whether it is a case of 'objectal' or 'narcissistic' depression, Eros or Thanatos – one finds in literature, art, and even religious fable 'a very faithful semiological representation of the subject's battle with symbolic collapse'. While such materials do not offer 'elaboration' in the sense of a 'becoming aware' of the precise causes of one's psychic condition (whatever it may be), they nevertheless possess 'a real and imaginary effectiveness that comes closer to catharsis than to elaboration'. For Kristeva, such representations act as a 'therapeutic device' used throughout human history and culture, one which differs from the psychoanalytic aim (where it arises) of 'dissolving the symptom'. Psychoanalysts, she argues, should 'enrich their practice by paying greater attention to these sublimatory solutions to our crises' in order, precisely, to be 'lucid counterdepressants' – perhaps not only for their patients, but for themselves too. Beyond therapeutic pessimism, psychoanalysis must confront itself as/with just such a 'counterdepressant'.

12

WALTER BENJAMIN

'PESSIMISM ALL ALONG THE LINE'

In 1929 Walter Benjamin published a critique of French surrealism, assessing the resources its legacy might offer for the task of thinking revolutionary politics.[1] For Benjamin, this entailed the re-evaluation of a Francocentric phenomenon from a German perspective (notably, one influenced by the forms of thought derived from German Romanticism), in order to go beyond the idea of surrealism as predominantly an artistic movement constituting 'the last trickle of French decadence' (47), as he puts it – that is, one devoted to esotericism, obscurity, and the primacy of aesthetic or 'poetic' experience over concerted political activity. (Such a perception, of course, overlooks those instances – close to the time of Benjamin's writing – where surrealism sought to break with its own orthodoxy in order to consider the revolutionary obligations it might indeed have.) Benjamin, however, detects in surrealist 'intoxication' (48) a political resonance as much as a purely pharmaceutical or ecstatic one. Surrealism is credited with uncovering the mystical yet radical potential of 'outmoded' cultural objects and practices: Benjamin speaks of the 'immense forces' concealed in these obsolescent forms which threaten at every turn to explode into 'revolutionary experience, if not action' (50). In this way, surrealism's techniques are radical in that they enable a 'political' rather than a merely 'historical view of the past' (50). Equally, however, it is only the possibility of revolt that allows surrealism to fully realize its creative or transformational potential. For Benjamin, then, the politicization of surrealism entails a dialectical movement whereby its innate hostility to bourgeois recuperation (through which it is viewed as essentially an aesthetic perspective derived from a 'contemplative attitude') drives surrealism to the left, connecting its concern with 'radical intellectual freedom' to the idea of 'revolutionary opposition' (52). Here, however, surrealism also takes severe issue with a 'well-meaning left-wing bourgeois intelligentsia' still heavily invested in 'traditional culture' and committed to articulating its 'political practice' in terms of 'idealistic morality' (53). The 'moralizing dilettantism' predicated on shallow notions of optimism and virtue that Benjamin detects in the bourgeois left is powerfully contrasted with 'the cult of evil as a political device' which connects surrealism to Dostoyevsky, Rimbaud and their like, who, decades earlier, were the surrealists *avant la lettre* of the late nineteenth century (53). Surrealism's politicization therefore marks that point at which insurrectional fervour refuses to be co-opted by the moralistic optimism of the bourgeois, social-democratic left.

If, however, surrealism rejects the 'sclerotic liberal-moral-humanistic ideal of freedom' in which radical struggle and suffering are effectively subjected to politico-theodical determination, the question remains whether the energies of surrealist revolt might ever angle themselves towards the 'constructive, dictatorial side of revolution', as Benjamin puts it (54), without which they presumably risk falling back into the pure esotericism of obscure self-referentiality (if only in the opinion of surrealism's detractors, or for that matter in the minds of its 'cultural' sponsors). The 'particular task' of surrealism, argues Benjamin, is not merely to register the 'ecstatic component' of each 'revolutionary act' but to somehow carry over its intoxicating anarchism into the problem of 'the methodical and disciplinary preparation for revolution' that is required if the surrealist gesture is not to lapse either into empty callisthenic exercises or effete self-congratulation (55).

For surrealism to avoid 'undialectical' mysticism or romanticism, therefore, it must establish a foothold in the 'everyday world'. What is avowedly 'mysterious' must nevertheless be powerfully secularized, so that radically new possibilities can be liberated from those objects and forms which are typical and familiar to the point of over-use and obsolescence:

> For histrionic or fanatical stress on the mysterious side of the mysterious takes us no further; we penetrate the mystery only to the degree that we recognize it in the everyday world, by virtue of a dialectical optic that perceives the everyday as impenetrable, the impenetrable as everyday. (55)

The secular politicization, via surrealism, of mysticism and its objects therefore leads to what Benjamin terms, throughout the essay, 'profane illumination'. By this means, surrealism is capable of what may be termed a political poetics, one which offers an alternative to the poetic politics of a moralistic left-wing bourgeois intelligentsia serving up merely 'a bad poem on springtime, filled to bursting with metaphors' that in their empty hopefulness substitute 'stock imagery' for actual emancipation (55). Decisively, and assertively, Benjamin names this brand of politics 'optimism'. In contrast, he echoes Naville's call for the 'organization of pessimism' (55), sensed in the 'particular task' of surrealism to angle revolt towards revolution. (For Naville, the 'pessimism' of surrealism should be construed in terms of a tireless effort harshly applied to its own objects, characteristic of the extreme endeavour to address that desperate epoch which called forth both Hegel and Marx: such pessimism is no more to be confused with serene philosophical scepticism than it is to be discovered through patient contemplation.) For surrealism to draw ever closer to 'the Communist answer' therefore entails, so Benjamin insists, 'pessimism all along the line', unbroken from start to finish (55).

To 'organize pessimism', for Benjamin, means to dispense with the 'moral metaphor' which, as Adorno following Nietzsche puts it, separates truth from reality through the negation that arises from the theologico-metaphysical projection of hope. (The imagery of hope, in other words, severs truth from reality in the present.) It means, instead, to 'discover in political action a sphere reserved one hundred per cent for images' (56), a sphere itself unbroken by the articulation of figures arising from moralistic or contemplative forms of discourse which in turn reinscribe social divisions (divisions they remedy in only a purely palliative sense). Far from privileging aesthetic experience as such, the revolutionary sphere of images to which Benjamin alludes therefore threatens the violent 'interruption' of many an 'artistic career' (56) in the cultural field, hitherto characterized by such divisive activity.

Thus, the revolutionary 'organization of pessimism' in the face of its 'optimistic' counterparts on the left (as much as in the face of capitalism itself) entails opening the sphere of images as one of 'universal and integral actualities'. Here, 'action puts forth its own image', joining political materialism with physical nature as a condition of the annihilating 'dialectical justice' of which surrealism itself promises to be an expression (56). Pessimism 'all along the line' enables the 'profane illumination' that initiates such a revolution, rather than merely revolt.

13

THEODOR ADORNO

'HURRAH-OPTIMISM'

In the seventy-third section of *Minima Moralia*,[1] itself composed mostly during the war from a position of exile in the United States, Adorno writes of 'the workers' movement' that its 'decay' is 'corroborated by the official optimism of its adherents' (113). While the founders of the movement shared certain reservations about its likely success, for Adorno the subsequent reinforcement of capitalism not only makes effective resistance harder but also causes its proponents to indulge unduly in sanguine expectation, the actual fragility of which is nonetheless indicated by a refusal to tolerate critique. While the 'consciousness of the masses' bears the indelible stamp of capitalist control, therefore, any attempt to alter this consciousness by 'withholding assent to it' is dismissed and condemned as 'reactionary'. In forbidding criticism of a 'proletariat' constituted as much as an expression of the system as its adversary, the 'optimistic' stance of workers' organizations thus only strengthens capitalism's hand. Preferring well-worn slogans to systematic analysis, left-wingers become entrenched in forms of behaviour that, while being as coarse as they are closed-minded, do not preclude intense sensitivity to the slightest doubt or faintest disagreement that might be encountered. Adorno finds this 'hurrah-optimism' reflected in the unquestioned assertion of 'international patriotism', based on dogmatic allegiance to an idea of the 'people' expressed through what Levinas, around the same time, termed the 'side-by-side' relation underpinning certain conceptions of sociality. Such 'frantic optimism', as Adorno calls it, distorts a recognizable yet now rather threadbare 'motif': 'the refusal to wait'. If dreams of political acceleration matching that of technological advancement eroded confidence in the less immediate historical process of 'public enlightenment', now such empty-shell confidence – theoretically bereft as it is – is left merely to restate 'belief in the power and greatness of the organization as such' (114). Thus, while individual action and spontaneity alike are renounced, blind hope in the 'masses, solidarity, Party, class struggle' prevails. For Adorno, such unjustified sentiment mirrors bourgeois optimism in its classical 'superstitious' form: 'look on the bright side', things will turn out alright in the end; and, perhaps most tellingly, '"The gentleman does not find the world to his liking? Then let him go and look for a better one"' (114–15). Thus is such trite sentiment, received from Enlightenment optimism and its theodical residues, transposed into the emancipatory language of the left, twisting it peculiarly out of shape.

Earlier in the text Adorno berates an unjust 'sociability' carried across from an empty affability, sure of its capacity to communicate with others, into the 'egalitarian spirit' itself (25–26). While 'casual', 'amiable' exchanges merely perpetuate 'silence', debasing both parties in the process, the intellectual expresses some measure of genuine 'solidarity' only by assuming the 'inviolable isolation' characteristic of contemporary existence.[2] Where 'social mixing and participation' imply identification with the (oppressed) other, such condescension entails a 'tacit acceptance of inhumanity'. 'To adapt to the weakness of the oppressed', writes Adorno, 'is to affirm in it the pre-condition of power, and to develop in oneself the coarseness, insensibility and violence needed to exert domination' (26). Even if aloof detachment risks bourgeois affectation as much as the expression of estrangement – 'distance from business at large is a luxury which only that business confers' – this inescapable 'entanglement' seems an unavoidable predicament the intellectual must negotiate in some fashion, rather than simply disavowing a certain degree of 'withdrawal' as merely the condition of the 'society' it seeks to negate (26–27).

From this perspective, mere 'solidarity' is as 'sick' as it is the 'most honourable' stance from a socialist point of view (51). Whereas once solidarity expressed in the Party form distilled the possibility of emancipation in a practical or tangible way so as to reduce or reconstitute the abstract generality of individual 'hope', the conspiratorial–purgatorial turn taken by Party politics breaks the specific contract of such solidarity by resurrecting in its very midst the abstract conception of the individual as potential deviant. Even as it licenses the opposition between true believers and defeatists or deserters, of course, this generality threatens desperately to subsume Party loyalty itself. Having taken this road, the Party does not bring to an end individual 'hope' but only radically perverts the form it takes. Perhaps unsurprisingly, then, Adorno writes later in the text: 'To think that the individual is being liquidated without trace is over-optimistic. For his cursory negation, the abolition of the monad through solidarity, would at the same time prepare the ground for saving the single being, who only in relation to the general becomes particular.' Hence, far from being eliminated, 'the things that history has condemned are dragged along dead' (135). Perhaps for this same reason, too, Adorno elsewhere suggests that 'when we are hoping for rescue`, a voice tells us that hope is in vain, yet it is powerless hope alone that allows us to draw a single breath' (121).

If the absurd vanity of hope is also what animates the living corpse of the modern individual, for Adorno it is Nietzsche who voices the strongest argument against not only theology but also metaphysics, namely that hope is mistaken for truth. What justifies this 'leap', as Adorno calls it? Our love of fate (*amor fati*) imprisons us, ensuring not only resignation and fantasy but also a certain distortion whereby hope-as-truth is 'wrested from reality by negating it' (98). Even the authentic critic or intellectual pins his hopes on posterity, in a way that is all too conformist in bourgeois terms. Nonetheless, by dint of another antithesis that more fully describes the position he finds himself in, to abandon hope altogether risks lapsing into blind dogmatism or, otherwise, 'cynical capitulation' on his part (100). Society, meanwhile, is clogged with 'paid propagandists', 'hired applauders' and other 'official agents of the cultural system' who are part and parcel of a social fraction bent on ensuring the legacy of current conventions, in pale imitation of a bygone Church. The empty benediction won from the future by such means, however, only condemns to oblivion all 'organized fame and remembrance', making of their proponents the already-dead. What is to be hoped for, in this context? It is left to the intellectual, upon learning that his 'secret motive' is 'illegitimate' – even if it is also indispensable on another score – to register the discovery (101). The duplicity of hope, which wrests truth from reality through negation, therefore also deeply marks the antithetical task of thought.

14

HANNAH ARENDT

'THE RIGHT TO EXPECT MIRACLES'

During the 1950s, in the wake of the publication of *The Origins of Totalitarianism*, Hannah Arendt planned two books which aimed, first, to reconsider the historical relationship of Marxism to the rise of totalitarian regimes of the twentieth century and, secondly, to provide an introduction 'into' politics. The latter was not principally conceived as a primer in political theory. Instead, it was to offer fresh access to political experience itself. In terms of the original conception of these projects, both were left unfinished. While Arendt's thoughts on Marx and Marxism were taken up in subsequent works, including *On Revolution*, the ideas surrounding an introduction 'into' politics culminated in works such as *The Life of the Mind* but also gave rise to a posthumously published volume, *The Promise of Politics*. The concluding essay of this volume, 'Introduction *into* Politics',[1] is based on material she presented during a lecture course at the University of California, Berkeley in early 1955.

Arendt contrasts hope and fear as the predominant and most striking components of the post-war political climate. Fear abounds at the looming threat of total destruction caused by the development of nuclear weaponry, and its usage as a means to end the conflict. Since what prevails is 'the fear that humanity could destroy itself through politics and through the means of force now at its disposal' (97), such fear is fear of politics itself (albeit based, for Arendt, on a distorted image of politics' actual meaning). Hope, consequently, is invested in the dream that politics – perceived as leading humanity to the very brink of annihilation – might be brought to a decisive end.

However, for Arendt, the idea that politics could be subsumed and cancelled through the rise of an apolitical, techno-bureaucratic state which resorted to administrative rather than political techniques to manage human affairs is plain terrifying as much as it is utopian. The absolute despotism of this government by 'nobody' is itself 'fearsome', writes Arendt – for who could lobby, address or reckon with this power exercised by 'nobody'? Thus, the real danger is not that politics continues after the protracted horrors of two world wars but, under the pressure of post-war sentiment, that it 'may vanish entirely from the world' (96) so as to pave the way for a new type of domination capable of perpetuating itself without recourse to 'political' means, and proving itself absolutely resistant to all forms of political opposition. We should most fear what we most hope for, in other words.

Impending termination of the possibility of political action is fearsome enough. Just as worrisome is a conception of freedom as freedom from politics, as if it were a positive resource discovered at the limits of the political itself. For Arendt, however, the very meaning of politics is freedom. (Later in the essay, she outlines the original Greek sense of politics as the exercise of freedom in the public space of the agora, undertaken as an end in itself rather than a 'political' means. For Arendt, however, this freedom was eroded by the establishment of the Academy as a haven from the agora itself. The Academy, in other words, became a place where one could be free from politics, whereas previously freedom was absolutely coterminous with politics. Once split off in this way from the public or 'political' realm, the idea of academic freedom therefore diluted the original sense of freedom as inherent to politics by effectively depoliticizing it, leaving the 'political' realm to suffer a long history of depoliticization passing through both religious and secular phases, themselves judged by the degree to which they tolerated freedom enjoyed in 'nonpolitical' spheres, and culminating in modern statist and latterly apolitical models of human government and sociality.) In light of the 'disaster politics' experienced throughout the first half of the twentieth century, the inclination to separate freedom from politics, which threatens political possibility itself, is matched by the post-war predicament of that form of politics based not on the exercise of freedom as an authentic expression of political experience, but rather upon the preservation of life as the principal function of the modern state. In the nuclear age, we are confronted by the desperate paradox that this form of politics supposedly devoted to human survival led to the development of a bomb so powerful that, while it seems to offer supreme protection to a domestic population through making possible the total obliteration of the enemy, actually potentialized – if not rendering inevitable – the utter annihilation of winner and loser alike. Thus, the rise of political forms and techniques at the state level construed in terms of the priority or necessity of safeguarding life leads, after Hiroshima, to the self-cancelling contradiction of post-war 'politics' and the risk of its banishment from the world. Once the bomb has been dropped, Arendt fears the catastrophic termination, once and for all, of politics' original fund of meaning.

But if what we most hope for is what we should most fear, is all hope then over? Is the seeming impasse surrounding this implosion of politics' meaningfulness quite beyond hope itself? Surmounting the apparently intractable difficulty encountered by post-war politics would seem to require a miracle. One might imagine that a thinker of Arendt's particular stripe would not hesitate to dismiss all talk of miracles as religious fantasy. On the contrary, she observes that we encounter 'infinite improbability' at every turn. From the very creation of the universe to the emergence of organic life, we are faced with the advent of things so absolutely 'unexpected, unpredictable, and ultimately causally inexplicable' that they are effectively miraculous. Indeed, for anybody who knows anything about the circumstances of human reproduction, each life is itself 'infinitely improbable'. More generally, pure natality (such as is found at each origin of the conditions of existence) is indeed miraculous when viewed 'from the standpoint of the processes it necessarily interrupts'. Bursting forth as the expression of 'demonstrably real transcendence', or of an unadulterated inventiveness whose conditions cannot be found in the objects or situations it invents, each genuinely new beginning in its very groundlessness 'corresponds to the religious transcendence of believing in miracles' (112). If the post-war predicament of 'politics' leaves, precisely, no grounds for hope, then in a modern age of miracles faith is perhaps better expressed as an irreducible faith in 'infinitely improbable' beginnings without ground. Indeed, if as Arendt suggests there is an indestructible element of prejudice that inevitably contaminates the untrammelled judgement found at the origin of genuine political action, then perhaps such a toxin might be carried over or converted into the very 'belief' that resurrects hope against hope. This would make a miracle worker of 'man' as the resolutely political animal he in fact is. And, indeed, Arendt says just this:

> The crucial difference between the infinite improbabilities on which earthly human life is based and miraculous events in the arena of human affairs lies, of course, in the fact that in the latter case there is a miracle worker ... The normal, hackneyed

word our language provides for this talent is 'action' ... [yet] action also marks the start of something, begins something new, seizes the initiative, or, in Kantian terms, forges its own chain. The miracle of freedom is inherent in this ability to make a beginning, which is inherent in the fact that every human being ... is himself a new beginning. (113)

The original meaning of politics handed down from antiquity, but brought to near-extinction by the modern age, is freedom and action along just these lines. Since politics construed in this way can only happen miraculously, as it were, the apparently hopeless predicament of post-war politics is not beyond answer. On the contrary, to 'expect miracles as a consequence of the impasse in which our world finds us' (114) leads us not away from fearsome political realities into misguided religious daydream or catastrophic apolitical fantasy, but instead – against all hope – towards the real meaning of the political once more. Just as the human being has a 'right to rights' as their very first or absolutely original right – something Arendt teaches us elsewhere – so, in a not unconnected way, we also have 'the right to expect miracles' (114). The idea that 'everything is political' is itself a prejudice of modern times: in terms of the original definition of politics set out by Arendt, many forms of human activity and behaviour are simply not 'political' at all, but signal a dilution rather than an enlargement of 'politics' in the proper sense. Yet while this assumption of all-pervasive politics results in both a widespread fear of the 'political' and the growing hope of its demise, for Arendt the prospect of a ubiquitous politics bent on its own destruction is countered by the thought of that perhaps incredibly unlikely yet miraculously incisive alternative which might counter the paradoxical depoliticization that accompanies such 'appalling' ubiquity in the first place (153).

15

SLAVOJ ŽIŽEK

HOPELESS COURAGE (WITH HEGEL AND BADIOU)

In *The Courage of Hopelessness*,[1] written to address the powerfully shifting political landscape that we navigate through increasingly well-worn reference points (Trump, Putin, Europe, Brexit, globalism, populism, terrorism and so on), Slavoj Žižek offers a short introduction to a series of wide-ranging commentaries which, in itself, constitutes perhaps the sole theoretical orientation for them. Žižek begins with a set of general reflections on the relationship between repetition and ending, inspired by Italo Svevo's 1920s novel *Zeno's Conscience*, a fictional (and self-consciously unreliable) memoir written at the behest of the protagonist's psychiatrist, and a tale much concerned with the tobacco dependency of the patient. Here, pivotally for the narrative, recognition that one is always free to quit smoking only prolongs the habit. In fact, knowing or telling yourself that you can stop at any time is what makes stopping not just unlikely or improbable but actually inconceivable within the paradigm of this form of thought, which imposes and re-imposes itself precisely in a way that guarantees continual deferral in each and every looming moment of decision. The very idea that you can stop, in other words, is what time and again raises the cigarette to your lips. Even more than the addictive properties of nicotine itself, it is the belief that one can quit which becomes habit-forming. Freedom of choice is in this sense falsely constituted, to the extent that it actually serves its opposite: non-freedom and non-choice. There is no option but to continue. No-one would begin smoking if this predicament was properly grasped from the outset, in the sense that nobody would choose to tolerate conditions defined precisely by an impossibly constituted hope of their ending (that is to say, by a hope which itself dreams of cessation only in service of an irremissible repetition). To put this in other terms, the hopeful expectation that one will change is exactly what obstructs change. It is, indeed, the very condition of possibility of repetition without ending. Since obviously this impasse promotes anxiety as much as relieving it, we arrive rather inevitably at the mise-en-scène fantasy of the last cigarette. Here, belief (that it will be over) dramatically intensifies with the idea that one is at an impending crossroads, an undeniable cliff-edge or a dizzying tipping-point – but, of course, since it is faith in an ending that maintains repetition in the first place, its intensification only intensifies the stranglehold. If anything, the supposed imminence of an ending makes it less, rather than more, likely. And so, the smoker smokes the last cigarette over and over again. Thus Zeno's analyst is forced to change course, concentrating on the pathology of the desire for ending rather than on quitting smoking itself. (In terms of its psychological primacy, needless to say, the former might continue in some fashion or other, even if the latter were to be achieved.)

Faced with this impossible dilemma, whereby the smoker's attitude to his habit cannot alter the fact of smoking one way or another, all hope seems to be lost. There is only guilt, despair, anxiety and desperate pleasure without real satisfaction. At this point, though, smoking becomes pointless (in precisely the sense that it continues whatever happens). And then it stops. These, indeed, are the only conditions under which it *can* end. The parable is clear enough. Whereas hope of change (whether distant or immediately pressing, deliberately calculated or passionately spontaneous) remains a key feature – indeed an operative element – of the status quo, it is only the fact of 'the total hopelessness of his predicament' that enables the addict to finally kick his habit. If it is a well-worn truism that bourgeois Leftists loudly advocate radical change not only to avoid its demands, but also to prevent it from actually happening, for Žižek we must go through this 'zero point' of the utter desolation of hope in order to fully grasp the revolutionary possibility of our current circumstances. If in politics, as in smoking, 'the possibility of change is evoked in order to guarantee that it will not be acted upon' (x), then the particular ideological flavour of what we might term 'hope-programmes' of every kind – from moderate to radical, reformist to revolutionary and accelerationist – is rather besides the point. Here, Žižek alludes to Giorgio Agamben's notion of 'the courage of hopelessness', offered in an interview with Jordan Skinner published online by Verso in 2014.[2] Žižek deems Agamben's 'insight' to be 'especially pertinent' at a time when 'even the most pessimistic diagnosis as a rule finishes with an uplifting hint at some version of the proverbial light at the end of the tunnel' (xi). For Žižek, therefore, the 'true courage' required of us today is

> not to imagine an alternative, but to accept the consequences of the fact that there is no clearly discernible alternative: the dream of an alternative is a sign of theoretical cowardice, functioning as a fetish that prevents us from thinking through to the end the deadlock of our predicament. (xi)

Agamben's actual remarks in the interview cited by Žižek are instructive. He first of all denies the pessimism frequently attributed to him – doubtless aware of the fact that, as Žižek himself notes, the most pessimistic analyses available are so conditioned by profound dissatisfaction with the present that they cannot resist fantasies of improvement or change. One might venture, indeed, that the pessimist is a radical optimist of sorts, although Agamben himself disputes the relevance of either optimism or pessimism in relation to 'thought' itself. Instead, like Žižek – but also following Marx – he suggests that it is 'the courage of hopelessness' rather than pessimism per se that exposes us to the possibility of revolutionary change. As Agamben puts it, 'radical thought always adopts the most extreme position of desperation', stripped utterly of the hope that resides deeply hidden within the pessimist's breast as much as it is worn ostentatiously on the optimist's sleeve. And yet, if 'thought' itself is equated by Agamben with just this 'courage of hopelessness', he cannot resist concluding that this constitutes 'the height of optimism' itself, which leads one to wonder whether such 'courage' can ever rid itself entirely of hope. In just a few short lines, Agamben quickly dispenses with both optimism and pessimism as concepts relevant to 'thought', and at the same time celebrates this heightened optimism as an effect of the hopeless courage he himself places at the heart of 'thought' itself. It certainly seems true that Žižek, like Agamben, puts all his hopes in this 'the courage of hopelessness'. Indeed, since it invests all its hopes in a hope beyond hope itself, doesn't this form of thinking redeem or redouble hope at the very point of its abandonment? Doesn't such courage therefore lack, as much as assume, the 'courage of hopelessness' which we are asked, perhaps despite ourselves, to wish or hope for? Is it ever truly possible to abandon all hope? If not, then surely the 'courage' Žižek advocates is hopeless in a double and indeed ironic sense, since for him only the utter desolation of hope will do the revolutionary trick. If an ineradicable supplement of hope – however small – threatens to scupper emancipation, then what are we to make of its textual traces in the thinking and writing of revolutionary 'courage'?

In Hegel's *Philosophy of Right*,[3] courage is described as a '*formal* virtue', in that it is 'a display of freedom by radical abstraction from all particular ends' (309). Neither the outcome of individual motives nor intrinsically 'spiritual' in nature, courage is less the characteristic of a specific subject than it is the general mark of an impact upon others. Courage, in other words, is in eye of the beholder, since 'the actual result' of courageous deeds on the part of an individual registers in the 'minds of others' and not necessarily in 'his own' (309). In an addition to the text, Hegel remarks that 'the mettle of an animal or a brigand, courage for the sake of honour, the courage of a knight … are not true forms of courage'. Instead, he argues:

> The true courage of civilised nations is readiness for sacrifice in the service of the state, so that the individual counts as only one amongst many. The important thing here is not personal mettle but aligning oneself with the universal. (309)

Since courage in the proper sense can only derive from collective action in service of the sovereign state, the true 'work' of courage is to actualize its final ends, and 'the means to this end is the sacrifice of personal actuality' (309). An essential part of this 'courage', through which it indeed realizes itself and achieves its true aims, is therefore the self-denial or even self-destruction of the individual as such. This courage would thus desolate the hope of the individual in a twofold and interrelated sense: the individual would not only jettison all particular hopes or wishes in favour of the collective 'work' of courage; but in precisely the interests of this self-same 'work', they would no longer hope for individuality itself. Hegel writes: 'The intrinsic worth of courage as a disposition of mind is to be found in the genuine, absolute, final end, the *sovereignty* of the state' (309). This end, the end of every individual in a double sense, would also seem to presage the absolute end of hope.

If one might think that this Hegelian conception of courage provides a way to imagine courage without hope, indeed without the possibility – or conditions of possibility – of hope, nevertheless it has not always been possible to conceive of radical courage so 'hopelessly'. Writing in *Le Monde* in February 2010 of the courage demanded by the present, Alain Badiou speaks of contemporary times as deeply 'disoriented', without the means to orientate our existence.[4] In the interests of this disorientation, rather than being judged for good or ill the past has instead been made wholly unreadable, in the process denying the orientation required to establish any future trajectory. The only ends are dead ends, Badiou suggests.[5] He therefore advocates a revitalized commitment to the readability of the past in the interests of re-establishing orientation. In turn this entails re-affirmation of the 'communist hypothesis'. What, Badiou asks, is this hypothesis? First of all, it consists in the 'egalitarian idea' that is itself devoted to overturning the 'common pessimistic idea, which once more dominates these times ... that human nature is doomed to inequality'. Orientation is thus sought in the overcoming of pessimism – not optimism and pessimism alike, whether as a dualism considered irrelevant to genuine 'thought', or as an alternative encountered only in the 'particular' (or by the individual) rather than in the dispassionate work of collective 'courage'. Next comes 'the conviction that the existence of a coercive, detached State is not necessary'. One must have the courage of one's convictions, for sure; but, equally, it is far from certain that such conviction can itself deaden rather than stir hope in the Hegelian sense. Perhaps one might be able to tie such conviction to the revolutionary consciousness which imagines the old 'self' already dead in service of the collective cause. But Badiou argues that the communist hypothesis establishes an orientation that nowadays must be operated 'personally' as well as 'collectively'. Indeed:

> The point is to minimally maintain a consistent subjective figure, without thereby having the support of the communist hypothesis which has not yet been reinstalled on a large scale. What is important is to find a real point on which to stand – whatever the cost may be – an 'impossible' point which cannot be inscribed within the law of the situation. We must have a real point of this kind and organize its consequences.

If, in Žižek's commentary on Svevo's novel, nothing less than the experience of pointlessness will prepare the ground for radical change, then Badiou's insistence on finding a 'point' must be treated carefully as not just the reversal or resistance of this logic. For it is an 'impossible' point nowhere locatable within the context that it aims absolutely to transform, and from which in a certain sense it derives none of its resources. If this 'impossible point' is in other words already 'outside' the situation it wishes to bring to an end, nonetheless it is also – and equally 'impossibly' – a 'real' point (and not, for instance, merely an ideal or transcendental one). It remains somehow concretely situated even if it utterly flouts 'the law of the situation'. Such a 'point' is still somehow a position, in other words, one from which to organize the possible consequences it brings about. If only through its rhetorical force, this last formulation does not sound like the 'not expecting anything' (xxi) approach which the radically shoulder-shrugging

Žižek adopts as his own prerequisite to hopeless courage. Badiou concludes:

> The main virtue which we are in need of is courage. This is not the case universally: in other circumstances, other virtues may be required as a priority. Thus, at the time of the revolutionary war in China, Mao promoted patience as a cardinal virtue. But nowadays it is courage. Courage is the virtue than manifests itself, regardless of the laws of the world, through endurance of the impossible. The thing to do is to maintain the impossible point without accounting for the situation as a whole: courage, inasmuch as it is a question of treating the point as such, is a local virtue. It arises from a local morality, and its horizon is the slow reinstallation of the communist hypothesis.

Here, then, courage is not oriented towards the universal in the same way that it is in Hegel. This is not to say that Badiou inverts Hegelianism to reinstate the particular nature of courage. Endurance, fortitude and courage at the point of 'impossibility' are critical to Badiou's 'communist hypothesis', but – since its defining mark is as yet unreadable in terms of the situation it finds itself in – that very same 'point' shorts out the circuitry of the particular and the universal, falling on neither side of the division or exchange that it impossibly re-marks. That said, since courage in Badiou's article is – by strict reason of the 'impossible' – not orientated purely towards the universal, one wonders whether the end of hope so decisive to the Hegelian-Žižekian vision of revolutionary change is fully possible here. If it is not, courage once more proves hopeless at being hopeless.

16

FRANZ KAFKA

'PLENTY OF HOPE, AN INFINITE AMOUNT OF HOPE – BUT NOT FOR US' (RE-READING WALTER BENJAMIN)

Walter Benjamin starts his famous essay written to commemorate Kafka ten years after his death with an anecdote that he indicates is itself Kafkaesque.[1] Later on, he offers another one. The first story concerns a certain aspiration, the last a curious wish. The use of anecdotal writing on Benjamin's part is well documented. Remarking upon the anecdote in texts by Benjamin and others, Peter Fenves outlines its main characteristics.[2] Anecdotes are conveyed – indeed, they hit home – in a way that holds something strangely in reserve. They deal in hearsay instead of evidence, received knowledge instead of first-hand experience. They are communicated not as testimony given from an eyewitness point of view; rather, they serve to retell that which – while typically having a more than familiar ring – cannot readily be verified or demonstrated as such. Indeed, in terms of their meaning or purpose, anecdotes are always rather indistinct and enigmatic, as if their access of truth somehow relies on an inscrutable quality that remains difficult to determine. If they do not rest on evidence, in other words, neither are anecdotes *self-evident*. They can no more be fully digested than they are capable of objective explication, so that they hesitate (yet, as it were, *resonate*) on the very threshold that marks passage from writer to reader, speaker to listener. Benjamin himself contrasts the effect of anecdotal writing with that of the empathetic identification conventionally encouraged by the journalism of his time, suggesting that anecdotes' resistance of normative contextualization renders them at once strangely present, somehow immediate in their unmediated form, and yet for the same reason just a little unplaceable. We are not drawn formulaically into their 'space', as happens with the contrivance of daily news stories, but rather they move compellingly and rather uncontrollably into ours, like an uncanny guest half-known of old.

What all of this adds up to, for Fenves, is that anecdotes depend on a certain deficit – and indeed negation – of authority. Lacking proper foundation, Fenves argues that 'under no condition can *auctoritas* express itself anecdotally' (153). However powerful they may be, authority cannot ultimately 'accrue' to anecdotes. Almost by definition, the anecdote remains in want of an original author. Even while their successful retelling inevitably increases the kudos of each narrator, anecdotes always lack an authoritative or 'proper' signature. Even if it aims at somehow overpowering its audience, the anecdote circulates in unregulated fashion. Its usage is certainly always motivated, but may nevertheless shift. Even as they invite a certain 'knowing' reception, anecdotes inevitably embarrass explanatory interpretation or expository reading.

It is perhaps no wonder, then, that – as in Benjamin's own commemorative essay – anecdotes sometimes deal with disappointed hopes or unfulfilled wishes. Giving with one hand

and taking with the other, theirs is a strange ethical, as much as textual, economy. The anecdote's power is as sublimely weak as it may be dramatically strong. Yet, in precisely its double or duplicitous marking, the anecdote is nonetheless – hope against hope! – capable of 'street insurgence', in Benjamin's own terms; as if the (self-) disruptive power of anecdotal insight, inasmuch as it resists authoritative conceptualization or dominating abstraction, accompanies the very potentiality of revolutionary change.

Benjamin's retrospective essay on Kafka begins with the tale of Potemkin, favourite of Catherine the Great, whose declining powers and worsening depression saw him lapse at times into a shamefully incompetent fug. If protracted, this risked severe dereliction of the Chancellor's duties, notably a steep pile of unsigned papers needing an official stamp. It falls to a minor clerk, Shuvalkin, to confront this miasma. Apparently unfazed by Potemkin's high office, he hounds the old man, taking advantage of the Chancellor's broken-down state to force his signature on every last document. In an apparently passive stupor, Potemkin obliges, and Shuvalkin proudly emerges to trumpet his success before a band of relieved dignitaries. But, on close inspection, every page is in fact signed 'Shuvalkin'. A seemingly tremendous coup is unmasked as merely shameful pomposity.

Precisely through the enigmatic quality of its comedy, the tale doubtless invites interpretation. If Shuvalkin wildly oversteps his place in order to restore lapsed authority on behalf of the state, his taking-control of the situation perhaps meets with a too literal response by the faltering incumbent. At precisely the moment authority seems both to shift and re-establish itself, are we to believe that the near-deranged Potemkin merely signs in the name of the now-actual representative of the state, the flunkey who has effectively taken over the Chancellor's responsibilities? In effect, that in a crazy way Potemkin does *precisely* what is asked of him, namely, to recreate the state's 'signature' afresh? Or is this act of counterfeited signing to be read ironically rather than literally? Is Potemkin's gesture actually one of desperate subversion in the face of his own disempowerment, expressing a fierce intolerance of insubordination that itself prefers the paralysis of state to the upstart pretensions of a clerk, regardless of whether they are well intentioned? Maybe so, yet we still can't avoid the suspicion that Potemkin is perhaps a little mad, at any rate not in his right mind (after all, his actions if intentional seem bent on crippling Russia itself), so that once more we find him literally incapable of signature, incapable of authoring or signing such an 'act' in his own right.

Whether he means to or not, either way Potemkin effectively derails authority by falsely signing it over. In a certain regard, the tale therefore makes for the perfect anecdote, one which nobody is able to sign. Choosing to compensate for the shortcomings of the powerful, rather than to seize the opportunity for change that is obviously much needed, the petty self-aggrandizing scheme of the underling is rewarded – deliberately or not – by a kind of aristocratic misprision that disturbs the workings of state perhaps all the more radically because it constitutes a subversive 'act' which cannot be signed for, that properly speaking cannot be assigned as such. Instead of an *act*, indeed, we witness the *event* of a certain historical overturning or discrediting of authority which, if not exactly fortuitous, nevertheless exceeds attributable intention on anybody's part. Does Shuvalkin aim to opportunistically undermine or authentically support Potemkin, and vice versa? The point – and power – of the anecdote lies in the very undecidability of the response. And, of course, 'witness' is no doubt the wrong term for our own reaction, our own standpoint, in relation to such a tale for which, precisely, no-one can sign, or counter-sign – except rather fraudulently.[3] 'Witness' implies an objective, dispassionate stance that would exculpate us from any involvement or implication in the anecdote we are given to read, whereas in fact the anecdotal form of the tale makes each one of us an uncertain part of its drama.

In view of this powerfully striking anecdote, therefore, the remark attributed to Kafka, to which Benjamin himself alludes, calls for careful re-reading: 'Oh, plenty of hope, an infinite amount of hope – but not for us' (113). For it implies not just that hope belongs to others while we ourselves must always despair – in other words, providing evidence of a radically pessimistic, tomorrow-never-comes sort of attitude on Kafka's part. Rather, the phrase itself may suggest that hope in its most fundamental sense is not subject to authoritative attribution or empathetic identification ('us'), but that its very conditions of possibility reside precisely in the overcoming or shattering of their sundry effects. For any 'hope' we might assign to either Potemkin or Shuvalkin is surely disappointed in the end, whether or not the clerk plans to serve or subvert the master, and whether or not Potemkin's semi-delirious penmanship seeks to further his own interests or those of the state (just as, throughout Kafka's writings, the experience of the law – if it may be called that – contrives the wretched comicality of personal hope). As this tragi-comic retelling of the master–slave relation indicates, hope emerges on the other – and not just the opposite – side of authority. And the anecdote is precisely the form in which this 'truth' can be somewhat enigmatically revealed.

Benjamin's other Kafkaesque anecdote, by the way, concerns what appears to be the lamentable and now obviously impossible desire of a fallen monarch turned ragged beggar, who in a wishing-game among strangers seems to rue the fact that he escaped his overthrow without even a good shirt. Narrating a scenario that comes to imply his own dramatic demise, the man's paltry wants in the here and now – a mere garment – capture perfectly the sense of his absolute desolation as well as, perhaps, the shallow trappings of sovereignty itself. But how pathetic that a beggar's fondest wish is that he should be a deposed king who kept his shirt! Perhaps, among this same company of strangers, we are all called to reflect on how impossibly backward-looking purely self-serving hopes may be, whether those of a hopeless down-and-out or an erstwhile or would-be prince.

17

JACQUES DERRIDA

HEGEL, BATAILLE, NEGATIVITY AND AFFIRMATION

The late 1960s makes it possible to juxtapose three very different writers – Jacques Derrida, Frantz Fanon and Hannah Arendt – at a particular moment in time. Derrida's 1967 essay 'From Restricted to General Economy: A Hegelianism without Reserve' appeared the same year that Fanon's *Black Skin, White Masks* was translated into English, while Fanon's reception in the Anglo-American world in the latter part of the decade (a time when Derrida was also securing his reputation internationally, notably via the United States) is evidenced by Hannah Arendt's essay, 'Reflections on Violence', published just two years later in *The New York Review of Books*. The latter contains several references to Fanon, who is by and large presented as exemplifying a growing taste for violent action, in vengeful response to forms of power construed as essentially 'violent'. Arendt disputes the intrinsic connection of power and violence, seeing violence as a symptom of power's disintegration rather than its ascendancy, and in turn she questions the effectiveness of violent resistance as a form of political action. Placing Fanon's text between those of Derrida and Arendt, it is possible to bring the three of them into a kind of dialogue – however awkward or uncomfortable it may be – because a key point of reference for each is the question of lordship and the master–slave dialectic in Hegel, bringing into focus issues about authority, power and violence. Through careful attention to the treatment of this vital intellectual resource in the works by these three authors, it is possible to show that Arendt's image of Fanon is reductive and inadequate when one re-reads him through the perhaps unlikely but nevertheless surprisingly rich prism of 'early' deconstruction.

In 'From Restricted to General Economy', first published in May 1967 in the French quarterly *L'arc* but subsequently included in *L'écriture et la différence* that same year, Derrida turns to the work of Georges Bataille, and to the question of its connection with Hegelian philosophy.[1] The essay is effectively the penultimate piece in this milestone publication – excluding the short text, 'Ellipsis', written especially for the volume, which closes the book. Following a broadly chronological order,[2] *L'écriture et la difference* (published in English translation as *Writing and Difference* in 1978) contains a series of writings published from 1963 onwards. In an interview with Henri Ronse that appeared in *Lettres francais* in December 1967, Derrida attempts to explain how the three major books published by him during that landmark year might be read in conjunction with one another, in the process offering an indication of how the various texts in *L'écriture et la difference* might themselves be connected. Leaving aside *La voix et le phénomène* for a moment (the third major publication of that year), Derrida suggests either that *L'écriture et la difference* might be pasted into the middle of *De la grammatologie*, so that the first section of the latter (where Derrida's grammatological notion of writing funds a deconstruction of logo-phonocentrism and the metaphysics of presence in Western thought, from classical philosophy all the way through to structuralism and linguistic science) could be considered prefatory to the collection; or, conversely, that *De la grammatologie* might be inserted at the very centre of *L'écriture et la difference*, which would position the last five essays of the latter volume (among them, 'From Restricted to General Economy') in terms of what Derrida calls a 'grammatological opening'. Here, the metaphysics of presence that orientate philosophy's treatment of writing would be opened or exposed to a powerfully deconstructive reading of its exclusions, restrictions, repressions, blind-spots and unacknowledged resources, pointing in the process towards an enlarged and transformed conception of writing within and against which the 'text' of philosophy is itself precipitated.

Since they appear to share a certain conceptual similarity or resonance, in 'From Restricted to General Economy' Derrida begins by comparing Bataille's notion of sovereignty with Hegel's conception of lordship. For Hegel, since servility may be understood in terms of a life which never puts itself fundamentally at risk, lordship as a type of freedom is attained at the point where life itself is fully ventured. This happens foremost through direct confrontation with death. Yet as Bataille himself saw, the passage towards lordship entails a repression of the 'slave' – the 'slave' *within* – in the identity-formation of the 'master', and thus a certain thraldom that redoubles itself in the very movement of transcendence. Moreover, somewhat paradoxically, lordship – as putting life at stake – is attained only by retaining the life one has hazarded. Perhaps most significantly, by endowing this process with a meaning inherent in its very constitution, 'the presentation of essence and truth' is maintained, serving as an indispensable stage in the formation of both 'self-consciousness and phenomenality', as Derrida puts it (254).

Life, then, is not absolutely ventured in lordship, and as such the freedom it entails is equally limited as the mere product of a 'ruse' (254) that subjects death to the meaning and truth of a consciousness bound to itself through a form of self-recognition which in fact only redoubles servile repression. In Derrida's terms, the partial or compromised freedom that may be associated with Hegelian lordship causes a 'burst of laughter' (255) in Bataille. The 'text' of Bataille laughs uncontrollably at Hegel's trademark of taking negativity seriously as foremost a philosophical 'resource'. Indeed, the explosion of laughter triggered by Hegelian philosophy promises an opening on to the 'other' that sovereignty may be, as distinct from the portentous gravity of lordship's salvaged or redeemed life. That lordship frees itself only by enslaving itself is the product of its dialectical formation, through which the play of negativity is, as Derrida notes, restricted and re-appropriated in the movement towards conservation and self-reproduction. Here, rather impossibly, death is merely 'reinvested' in life as an asset, part of its economy of resources. In contrast, sovereignty for Bataille emerges beyond (albeit not exactly outside) the work of dialectics, risking absolute and profitless expenditure of life, consciousness, seriousness, presence and meaning in the interests of a more radical or unreserved freedom which may be reduced neither to the subordination of the slave nor to the retention of an existence whose venturing is somewhat of a 'ruse'.

Derrida explores sovereignty's relation to an ecstatic, poetic or sacred form of speech that not merely opposes or sacrifices 'significative discourse' (such discourse would seem to affront sovereignty in its servile commitment to seriousness[3]), but which perhaps opens itself as the more original economy within which dialectics – as a type of restriction, compromise or 'economizing' – finds its resources. This, indeed, is why dialectics is not just extrinsic to sovereignty, but instead may be understood as a precipitous reaction to a 'negative side' which in fact 'can longer be called negative' to the extent that it refuses to provide the resources for positive 'conversion' in the interest of meaning or truth: a 'sovereign' negativity, in other words, that simply does not permit the stable distribution of positive and negative poles. In these terms, sovereignty is not merely the inverse of Hegelian lordship or dialectics, but might rather be construed as whatever flouts, undermines or upsets the very thinking of difference as located in oppositional terms which may be recuperated according to the given hierarchies established by an entire metaphysics of essence, truth and meaning. Sovereignty, we might say, is another name for a more radical difference no longer in the service of presence or signification.

As the essay develops, Derrida discusses the relation of sovereignty to writing. On the one hand, sovereignty objects to the servility of writing. It does so, not merely in the sense of the Platonic tradition's disdain of writing as extrinsic, auxiliary and inanimately technical in relation to living speech. Rather, sovereignty mistrusts writing (in, let us say, its significative or dialectical forms) as that which in fact *serves* the life which wishes to retain itself as presence. On the other hand, however, the more original or general economy opened up by Bataille's thinking of (an always non-present) sovereignty relates to Derrida's own conception of the trace structure of writing – writing in the enlarged sense – that forms the interest of much of his work from this period. Thus, even at the point that Hegelian philosophical discourse, by putting negativity earnestly to work, bets against 'play' or 'chance', it simultaneously puts itself *into* play as an 'interpretation submitted to an interpretative decision', serving therefore as an '*inscription*' as much as a '*knowledge*'. The meaning of the Hegelian text, the meaning derived from it, is henceforth no more or less than a '*function* of play' precipitated by the more general economy that remains irreducible to the restrictive operations it desires. Sovereignty does not suppress, subordinate or transcend dialectics, which would merely reduce it to an effect of dialectics. Instead, it 'provides the economy of reason with its element, its milieu' (260–61) – in other words, the (albeit groundless) grounds of its 'play'. Equally, then, traces of sovereignty found in poetic, ecstatic or sacred forms do not give rise to just another discourse than the 'significative' – all discourse is 'significative', affirms Derrida – but instead they constitute that which *in every discourse* may open up the possibility of play or chance. Such play is likened to a type of sliding which is itself chancy, since it always risks sliding into meaning: 'It risks making sense, risks agreeing to the reasonableness of reason, of philosophy, of Hegel, who is always right, as soon as one opens one's mouth to articulate meaning' (263). Yet to run this very risk is doubtless also what makes 'play' what it is; although, far from abandoning it to the unforeseeable effects of pure randomness, Derrida suggests that for Bataille sovereign language calls for ruses, stratagems, masks of all kinds. Play must risk intention as much as meaning, it seems, even if such risk is deeply complicated by all the 'simulacra' and 'silences' of its 'milieu'. Sovereignty not so much adopts 'the position of non-sense', but rather traces out the 'affirmative reduction of sense' within the general economy or enlarged space of 'writing' or inscription (269). It is not simply 'transgressive', to the extent that transgression tends to 'conserve or confirm that which it exceeds' (274), but neither for Derrida is it just 'neutral', since that term, too, is itself readily available for recuperation within an entire series of oppositional pairings that provide philosophy or reason with its traditional resources. Sovereignty, if there is any, affirmatively marks the 'play' that writing precipitates and contends with.

Not a thing in itself, for Derrida sovereignty of the Bataillean stripe tilts asymmetrically, moves baselessly, slides into and across language, threads through it, without gravity: 'the chain rest on nothing' (274). The – albeit constitutive – violence that sovereignty does to writing matches the shaming farce of recognition it exposes in lordship. As Derrida writes, 'The sovereign renunciation of recognition enjoins the erasure of the written text' (265). Lordship as a form of mastery is therefore just another name for the repression of writing that characterizes the 'text' of philosophy, the hysterical travesty of its self-recognition, the redoubling catastrophe of servitude.

18

FRANTZ FANON

RECOGNITION AND CONFLICT

One of the latest pieces in *Writing and Difference*, at least in terms of date of publication, Derrida's essay on Bataille and Hegel is followed in the collection by 'Structure, Sign and Play in the Discourse of the Human Sciences', a text which, whether or not written earlier, was famously presented the previous year at the Baltimore conference at Johns Hopkins in 1966; a paper and an event that helped to cement Derrida's reputation in the Anglo-American academy. If, in hindsight at least, *Writing and Difference* feels like a book that tracks the trajectory which led Derrida from qualified recognition in France to international acknowledgement and ultimately cultural celebrity, beginning first and foremost in America, then during the same year the translation into English of another major work by a very different writer (albeit one with an equally fraught and highly complex relationship to French colonialism) represents another singular example of the traction that may be gained through positive reception in the United States. Against the backdrop of the civil rights movement and other progressive and revolutionary trends in the late sixties, while Frantz Fanon's *Black Skin, White Masks* (as well as other writings by him) had obviously enjoyed circulation and influence outside of the francophone world prior to 1967,[1] its impact undeniably increased, with a growing militant trend in Fanon scholarship making itself felt, and a number of biographical and critical studies appearing in the years immediately after the late 1960s,[2] whose influence was foremost in the Anglo-American world. During the decade after his death, Fanon had become a greater symbol of African anti-colonial struggle (some of the earlier Anglo-American scholarship reflects this), but by the time *Black Skin, White Masks* was translated into English, it is fair to say that in France and Algeria Fanon's significance was not huge, even during periods of civil unrest and political resistance.

However, Fanon's work drew – however singularly – on forms of 'Western' critical thought that key sections of the Anglo-American academy immediately recognized and enthusiastically debated at this time, in particular psychoanalysis, Marxism and their antecedents. In 'The Negro and Recognition',[3] for instance, the penultimate chapter of *Black Skins, White Masks*, the Hegelian theme of mutual recognition as the origin of man's self-consciousness and potential freedom is tested against the complex circumstances to which colonialism leads, so that the problematic of lordship, mastery and servility in Hegel which Derrida explores through his own reading of Bataille is here given a further twist along its historical axis (albeit that the question of what constitutes our sense of history is as much asked as it is answered in this treatment). 'The Negro and Recognition' begins, in fact, with a discussion of Adlerian psychology, but then finds its central point of reference in Hegelian discourse. Since for Hegel the possibility of self-knowledge originates in the process of identifying an object of desire, in terms of which one can distinguish and thus experience oneself as such, the 'other' by whom I need to recognize myself must be independent and enduring rather than simply immediate or fleeting, if the knowledge of the 'self' thereby attained is not merely transitory or superficial (as the fulfilment of desire can frequently be). This other must therefore be like me: another self-consciousness in which I recognize myself. Such recognition establishes, in turn, the possibility of a community based on mutual self-recognition. However, since one's recognition as an independent self-consciousness also relies upon a display of detachment or freedom in which one's life may be put at stake, the possibility of community or indeed mutuality derives from a fateful and potentially fatal encounter with the other. During such a struggle, the risk is that both winner and loser lose: the latter, because failure means destruction; the former, because victory puts to an end the other who in fact establishes the very conditions of possibility for one's own self-recognition. Such a potentially dead-end form of mortal combat is thus recast by Hegel in terms of the living relations of master and slave. Here the conflict between the two is, ostensibly, somewhat redeemed or resolved. The master is granted superiority, freedom and independence, while the slave is given a reason and position by which to live, namely servitude in relation to another. However, the recognition that the slave affords the master – insofar as it does not stem from another self-consciousness like me, but rather from one who has pulled back from staking his life, and settled instead for passive servility – proves as unsatisfactory as that of a fatally vanquished opponent. The pursuit of desires which itself grants the possibility of knowledge or consciousness of 'self' in the first place is, meanwhile, dimmed by the presence of the slave, whose work on the master's behalf not only places the latter in a paradoxical situation of dependency but also interrupts the relation to the objective world that furnishes the possibility of desire's satisfaction. As we have already observed, therefore, ultimately the slave affords the master neither true self-consciousness nor independence. True recognition, it follows, must be fully mutual rather than one-sided and unequal, although needless to say achieving such an outcome is far from an uncomplicated matter, given the paradoxical consequences of the original circumstances of Hegelian recognition that give rise to the master–slave relation in the first place. As Derrida points out, it is sovereignty in Bataille's sense that exposes recognition to its own constitutive contradictions and lays bare the deconstuctibility of its 'text'.

In 'The Negro and Recognition', however, the Hegelian theme of mutual recognition as the origin of man's self-consciousness and possible freedom is not so much philosophically deconstructed (at least, not at first glance), as it is tested against the complex circumstances to which colonialism has led us, or rather against the interpretation this situation affords. In the second subsection entitled 'The Negro and Hegel', Fanon begins by stating that there is no 'open conflict between white and black'. Instead, the 'Negro slave' is 'recognized' by the 'White Master' in a situation that is '*without conflict*' (217). A few sentences later, returning to the theme of the master's recognition of the slave which he once more states occurs without 'struggle', Fanon suggests that, to the extent that the 'Negro' has been liberated from slavery without having to engage in mortal combat for his freedom, the grounds of the relationship between the two have not fulfilled their Hegelian destiny. The 'Negro' has neither properly cast off the shackles of slavery nor acquired anything more than a paltry semblance of mastery. In the process, the 'White Master' attains a certain personhood by recognizing the other without entering into full conflict, but lacks genuine consciousness of the 'self' he truly is (219). Given these subsidiary comments, one may surmise that the lack of 'open conflict between white and black' to which Fanon refers is due principally to the historic evasion he attributes to slavery's ending.[4] Yet elsewhere in his writing Fanon also implies that the relations between 'black' and 'white' are not reducible to the master–slave dialectic; indeed, that the state of affairs we call colonialism arises in circumstances that are, in essence, not defined by original combat of the internecine kind that founds the possibility of the master–slave relation. Of course, for Hegel himself, such combat is never simply a 'natural' occurrence, depending as it does on a specific detachment of the 'self' from the 'nature', and thus it always acquires a historicality beyond some intrinsic necessity. Nonetheless, it is far from clear that Fanon uniformly or uncritically accepts its extension in the interests of a wholesale explanation of colonial history. From this perspective, the idea that the 'Negro slave' is 'recognized' by the 'White Master' in a situation that is 'without conflict' may acquire a double meaning: more overtly, that the colonial situation 'post-slavery' ushers in something like a phony war; but perhaps more suggestively, that colonialism's historical interpretation is in fact not drained dry by the Hegelian logic of master–slave. And, on the basis of this double reading or double possibility, one is left asking whether, in Hegel's aftermath, it is historical *interpretation* or the historical *process* itself that is broken or has gone awry, notably in terms of what we understand by the 'colonial'.[5] Such a double possibility implies not just the risk of interpretative conflict or combat, but a potential re-creation of the conditions of mastery and servitude that define the stakes of this fraught, ambivalent or divided situation. Here, in Derridean vein one might re-evoke Bataillean sovereignty as that which intervenes between the two 'sides', deriding and degrading in each case the bid for self-recognition that *in a double sense* occurs at the expense of the 'other', but which also exposes to its own deconstructibility the very 'text' of the 'colonial' whose inscribed divisions are so frequently placed under erasure. To the extent that the 'text' of Fanon resists resolving too neatly the double and divided possibilities it exposes, the resistance of 'erasure' that Derrida equates with the moment of sovereignty is surely – if perhaps surprisingly – resonant in his work.

Be that as it may, for Fanon the 'former slave' nevertheless seeks recognition of the Hegelian kind. Following Hegel, for Fanon such recognition can only occur through a mutuality which must be humanly constructed since it relies on a certain disconnection of self-consciousness from 'nature', but one which at the same time has to transcend given human distinctions since it implies 'the universal consciousness of self'. Fanon writes: 'Each consciousness of self is in quest of absoluteness. It wants to be recognized as a primal value without reference to life, as a transformation of subjective certainty (*Gewissheit*) into objective truth (*Wahrheit*)' (217–18). Nonetheless, as desire meets resistance from the other – such resistance providing the essential ground for true self-consciousness to emerge – the pathway 'toward a supreme good that is the transformation of subjective certainty of my own worth into a universally valid objective truth' (218) seems bound to lead to conflict and violence. In order to achieve recognition – i.e. to 'do battle' for a newly created 'human world' of 'reciprocal recognitions' – the black 'former slave' must, it seems, venture his life in a 'savage struggle' against the one who is reluctant to recognize him fully (218). And yet surely the Hegelian 'truth' of this situation – the radical possibility of overcoming the historic evasion Fanon associates with the end of slavery – is at the same time countermanded by the possibly *extrinsic* relation of the master–slave dialectic to the historical interplay between 'white' and 'black' to which he elsewhere alludes. This ironic possibility affects not only the question of the status – both conceptual and strategic – of violence in Fanon's discourse (since it does a kind of violence to the call for violence), but once more raises the problem of what exactly obstructs decolonization; whether the fault lies in the interpretative shortcomings of 'theoretical' constructs and arguments that largely belong to a European tradition, or in contingent facts and constraints that might impede or alter their implementation or translation on the ground. If the strength of the Fanonian 'text' derives in a certain way from the radical affirmation of a seemingly impossible task – namely to imagine the chance of a decisive break from the conditions of guilt, self-loathing and psychological violence which Fanon like every 'man of color' inherits, when those very same conditions seem inescapably to embody and define the possibility of living or being in the world[6] – then the traction gained through refusing to place under erasure this very impossibility (as also constitutive possibility) amounts to a kind of explosive violence against lordship, albeit a violence that enjoins violence *otherwise*, against itself in a certain way.

19

HANNAH ARENDT

VIOLENCE AND POWER

Such an impossible affirmation is evident not only in *Black Skin, White Masks*. Fanon's *The Wretched of the Earth* equally asks us impossibly to reconcile, on the one hand, a call to arms in which colonial adversaries are imagined to be locked in Manichean relations of frontal opposition, and, on the other, a set of psychiatric studies and observations that not only put in doubt presumptions about the possibility of such clear-cut distinctions in the embodied experience of colonial subjects, but which leave largely unresolved the question of how one gets from the deeply ambivalent conditions exemplified by the pathological behaviour of Fanon's patients – all of whom endure the complex legacy of psychic violence that connects as much as separates 'colonizer' and 'colonized' – to the pure and absolute confrontation willed at the level of the revolutionary acts of decolonization, or, for that matter, to the single form of universal 'man' that he depicts as constitutive as much as ideal.

Further evidence of the impact of Fanon's work upon the Anglo-American critical scene in the late 1960s is found in Hannah Arendt's lengthy special supplement published in *The New York Review of Books* in February 1969, 'Reflections on Violence',[1] which not only cites *The Wretched of the Earth* on several occasions but also establishes various allusions to Fanon's writing in the context of what Arendt sees as a false connection between violence and power at this time. For Arendt, the intensification of violence and of the means of violence throughout the twentieth century, brought about in large part by rapid technological developments, disrupts any simple equation whereby violence may be construed as just a means to political ends. Since the extreme violence made possible by advancements in technology can be co-opted by weaker or smaller powers, she suggests with some prescience that violence at least in its narrow sense may increasingly become the recourse and preserve of the powerless rather than simply the normative instrument of the powerful. Such a situation, indeed, implies for her a certain 'reversal' in the relationship between violence and power. Moreover, for Arendt the increasing politicization of violence by the Left during the 1960s overlooks the fact that from a strict Marxist perspective power is overcome or challenged not by violence per se but because of its own inherent contradictions as they are played out in historical and material terms. The violence that arises in class struggle is therefore not the fundamental cause of radical change but only an effect of the deeper forces that condition or provoke it. Among her contemporaries, Sartre is one of the most prominent targets in this critique of a new 'shift' towards violence within revolutionary thinking. It is as if, from Arendt's viewpoint, the Left have succumbed to a disastrous fascination with violence that characterizes the twentieth century, whereby overt pacifism and extreme resistance to violent means has yielded, by dint of a relatively undisturbed inversion, to its militant glorification. Vengefulness sullies the desire for revolutionary transformation; fantasies of violent purification impede rational analysis and action; uprisings based solely on such 'mad fury' actually jeopardize the possibility of lasting victory or enduring change.

Obviously Arendt does not simply advocate strict Marxism as the answer for a critical or Leftist position, far from it, and in this essay she is highly critical of several of its key theoretical components, not least the doctrinal commitment to progress that Marxism shares with many other forms of thought within the Western tradition.[2] It is in this respect, in fact, that Marxist thinking may be used to support as much as question the recent taste for revolutionary violence. As a form of action that may be considered to intervene in the historical process, it might be deemed a force for the provocation or acceleration of change as much as one that risks distorting or perverting historical outcomes. But, for Arendt, to the extent that violent action is within contemporary Leftist discourse largely construed in terms of the destruction of the old (being, for her, squarely at odds with forms of action devoted single-mindedly to the creation of the new), its position within political debates current in the late 1960s is open to important criticisms.

In fairness, in advancing these criticisms of a growing taste for revolutionary violence, Arendt does not merely overlook the distinctions between various thinkers and writers of the time. Instead, for example, she suggests that Fanon is at least more in touch with 'reality' than other intellectuals who irresponsibly glamorize violence. However, her key contention remains that the conception of power based predominantly on its capacity for coercive force or the threat of warfare is as badly flawed as the advocacy of revolutionary violence as a solution to the supposedly inherent 'violence' of power. Indeed, she points to bureaucracy as the modern form of power that is perhaps most tyrannical of all, implying that its basis is in a certain respect non-violent. This proposition, it might be argued, holds weight only on the strength of the narrowest definition of violence, although equally Arendt's conception of power as organizational and productive

or non-repressive as such resonates with emerging paradigms
of thought in this period, for instance in the thinking being
developed by Foucault. Arendt points to the ancient and modern
traditions of civil government as entailing a notion of power
that is not so crudely aligned with the command–obedience
relationship that equates power with the capacity for forceful
coercion. Such traditions base themselves, instead, on the idea
of consensual submission to laws established by some form of
representative government. For Arendt, the power derived from
models of civility depends to a significant extent on a certain
strength of numbers, one that purely violent domination may well
forego (given the right instruments of violence, she argues, a
very few can hold dominion over a great many). While Arendt
seems to appreciate that such distinctions are not merely clear-
cut, her argument is that they do point to the need for greater
differentiation within a family of terms which, at the time, were
too readily conflated: powers, strength, might, authority and
violence, as she lists them. This is especially true, she argues,
when one considers the question of revolution. Revolutions
are not won or lost on the strength of violence, but succeed
or fail depending on how far power has broken down. Thus,
revolutionary violence – to the degree it seems effective – is
merely symptomatic of a disintegration of power. That the two
are related in this way makes them far from identical. On the
contrary, violence intensifies where power lessens. Furthermore,
Arendt argues that since such breakdowns of power are not
dependent on an upsurge in violence, they may – and do –
occur without it. It is the superior organization of power rather
than superior means of violence than establishes the rule of the
master. While violence is a means to an end, power is neither;
not simply an instrument nor a goal in itself[3] but instead 'the
very condition that enables a group of people to think and act

according to means and ends', as Arendt puts it. Violence may threaten or damage power, but it cannot in and of itself result in power.

It is at this point in the essay that Arendt writes: 'To substitute violence for power can bring victory, but its price is very high, for it is not only paid by the vanquished, it is paid by the victor in his own power.' This sounds very much like the quandary of lordship, one we have traced both in Derrida's treatment of Bataille and Fanon's reading of Hegel, whereby the division of master from slave excludes the possibility of sovereignty.[4] However, that Arendt sees an intimate connection between violence and lordship provokes an insight about sovereignty as we have discussed it. If it is violence that restricts sovereignty in the very form that lordship takes, then sovereignty even if violent is not reducible to violence, since it must also oppose or exceed violence in a certain way. Sovereignty would entail not only a violent reaction to servile mastery but, also and at the same time, a 'violent' reaction to the violence that results in lordship. This double violence, including the resistance of violence to itself, is something that – with the help of Derrida's reading of Bataille on Hegel – we have been able to detect in Fanon's work, which as we have seen does violence to the call for violence at the very moment it refuses to place under erasure the double and deconstructible writing or 'text' of colonialism. This would imply that 'violence' in Fanon is not reducible to Arendt's description of the contemporary taste for violent responses to power's presumed 'violence', even if one 'side' of Fanon is highly recognizable in these terms. There may be, as we have suggested, a 'sovereign' violence in Fanon's writing which also does violence to such violence.

In the latter stages of the essay, reversing the more positive note she strikes in alluding to him several pages earlier, Arendt reverts somewhat to listing Fanon among a group of authors who glorify violence[5] and who seek vengeance rather than justice, even if such retribution risks chaos and self-destruction. Fanon is charged with promoting the dangerous impression that the 'antipolitical' desolation of individual death may be converted, through the collective hazarding of life in violent struggle, into an experience of transcendence over mortality. She goes so far as to suggest that Fanon equates violence with vitality or the force of life itself. For Arendt, however, this quasi-Hegelian idea of a redemptive, fraternal rebirth 'actualized only under conditions of immediate danger to life' can have no lasting political future. Not only is its appeal shallow and transitory, but by equating vitality with violence it connects to 'the most pernicious elements in our oldest tradition of political thought', a tradition which interprets power itself (whether in state or other form) in organic or biological terms, in the process re-establishing the fallacious identity of power and violence. As a result, both power and its resistance or overcoming boil down to violence, with disastrous consequences. For Arendt, this way of thinking is ultimately non-political in character. Even though it has obvious ideological attributes – ones that, as she notes, are powerfully harnessed where racism in particular is concerned – it misses the question and possibility of politics in the strict sense. (To the extent that the 'politics' of race goes down such roads, Arendt suggests, it is destined to forgo the chance of properly 'political' action or resolution.)

Arendt's arguments about distinguishing violence from power may be convincing up to a point, and doubtless it would be interesting to pursue the possible relationship of this non-coercive conception of organizational power with not only Foucault's developing body of work but an array of 'political' writings of the time. Of course, the contrast between her idea of power as essentially 'nonviolent' and the thought of sovereignty as that which does violence to the violence of servile mastery implies political possibilities that could go in rather different directions. However, the main purpose of this chapter has been to show that, on Arendt's own terms, Fanon cannot be reduced to a figure of 'violence' as she understands it, and that we are able to arrive at this understanding by re-reading Fanon with Derrida's article on Bataille and Hegel in the background. That all of the texts considered here – chosen somewhat deliberately for their very obvious differences – share both a certain reliance upon and a certain questioning of the Hegelian inheritance suggests not only its complex currency within late 1960s 'critical' or 'political' discourse. Reading across the borders of these texts, we are also challenged to reconsider how we approach the question of the relationship between violence and resistance today, both in thought and in action.

20

ÉTIENNE BALIBAR

POLITICS AND PSYCHOANALYSIS

Drawing upon psychoanalysis, how might one think of the relationship between psychological states or conditions, on the one hand, and political forms and practices, on the other? What resources does psychoanalysis offer for conceptualizing either the psychological dimensions of the 'political' or, for that matter, the 'politics' of the psyche, especially in their collective or social instantiations? For many years, these have been enormous questions for those working in various fields of the humanities wanting – in different ways and at different times – to articulate psychoanalytic interpretation with political theory. Looking at the writings of Étienne Balibar, one particular response to such questions is to interrogate, in a short yet dazzling text included in the recently published volume *Citizen Subject*, the Freudian conception of the super-ego, notably in its development during the early 1920s.[1]

Before we come to this essay, however, originally presented on the 150th anniversary of Freud's birth (and in an amphitheatre named after Freud's teacher Jean-Martin Charcot), it is worth situating the interactions it provokes between politics and psychoanalysis in terms of Balibar's larger project, if it may be called that. A key point of departure for many of his writings is,

of course, the enduring question of citizenship, dealt with in a
range of influential texts including those found in *We, the People
of Europe?* and *Equaliberty*. Citizenship is obviously both an
abiding and a recursive or iterative problem for political thought.
It arises in many contexts, not least of which is the question of
Europe in all its senses; but it also imposes itself through the
far from unrelated – though not simply identical – issue of world
populations in flux, the relationship between the 'local' and the
'global', and so on. Needless to say, these questions have
been powerfully renewed in more recent times, under different
yet connected conditions and circumstances, making the 2015
English publication of Balibar's Wellek lectures,[2] almost a decade
and a half after their original delivery, as well as the recent release
of collections like *Citizen Subject*, also prepared over many years,
far more timely than belated. The publication of such titles, in
other words, reopens the question: Whither citizenship? Given the
rising instance and intense complications of statelessness and
forced migration worldwide (not to mention travel bans imposed
recently by the United States), given the finance politics that, in
Balibar's own terms, make Europe an 'apartheid' of sorts,[3] given
the increasing privatization of public and welfare provision as an
example of the erosion of what citizenship means in its practical
as well as ideological sense, given the ongoing transformation of
the various relationships of nation-states to the private interests
of multinational companies (and, for that matter, the transnational
social and economic effects of certain nation's or groups of nations'
fiscal policy on the world's stage), given the far-reaching effects
globally of debt capitalism, given the intensifying lack of separation
between the political and economic spheres that would seem to
mark the transition from liberal democracy to neoliberalism,[4] given
the impact of certain nationalisms and fundamentalisms of various
types over the past decades, given the politics of security and

'counter-terrorism' that affects rights of all kinds – given all of this, what is to be made of citizenship today?

The contribution made by Balibar's Wellek lectures to the critical thinking of citizenship, civility and violence today is as undeniable as the impact of his many other writings. A word is due about the role played by psychoanalysis throughout these lectures, however, one that if anything seems to have intensified rather than diminished during that long editorial period between their original presentation and final publication. While it would be wrong to say that the entire thesis is explicitly framed and developed through continual recourse to psychoanalytic concepts, arguments and ideas, nonetheless I would argue that in crucial ways the 'psychoanalytic' is resorted to, albeit through a deliberately transformative gesture, as a vital resource for the *form* of thinking that Balibar deems necessary in relation to his subject matter. In particular, the 'limits' of political philosophy alluded to in the book's subtitle are arguably traced out through a distinctively *resistant* relationship to psychoanalysis which amounts neither to a rejection nor a critique, but which instead exploits the resistances *of* psychoanalysis in the interests of the most relevant questioning concerning the 'political' today.

Obviously the question of violence is a key motif for the particular project of these lectures. At a number of points in the published text, as he re-engages the legacy of Freud, Balibar considers the idea of a 'cruelty or capacity for destruction' that is located beyond the Freudian death drive itself, in order that he might re-think extreme types of violence which exceed the forms of authoritarianism, domination and oppression that are familiar within the historic arc of the nation-state. This 'beyond' tips over instead into a violence that stems from an *'idealization of hatred'* (perhaps more and more recognizable today), which Balibar considers in terms of an extension or transformation of fascism beyond its 'ordinary' or state form (59–60). The reference point for the theoretical possibility of such a mutation in the conceptual toolkit of Freudian psychoanalysis is, interestingly, Derrida's essay, 'Psychoanalysis Searches the States of Its Soul: The Impossible beyond of a Sovereign Cruelty', which was presented as an address to the States General of Psychoanalysis held at the Sorbonne in 2000 (four years after the Welleck lectures were originally delivered, hence my remark above). Thus the thinking of violence in its contemporary guises comes to entail, for Balibar, critical re-engagement with psychoanalytic concepts, categories and forms of thought in the broader sense. In particular, through the reference to Derrida, it is clear that an understanding of sovereignty in its current manifestations (operating as a shifting ground as much as a stable phenomenon) benefits from this critical interaction or alignment. Importantly, however, the grounds of psychoanalysis are themselves transformed in the process. Picking up once more on Derrida's evocation of 'the beyond of the death drive', for Balibar the latter entails 'the dissociation of the tension or "unity of opposites"' between life and death, resulting in drives which we must recognize in terms of the modern principle or contemporary problematic of sovereignty itself. Balibar writes:

> This no longer has anything to do with the psychological analogy of ill-will or human 'evil'; the hypothesis is, rather, that the constitutive association of death with life is turned back against life itself, inverting the function of defense of the 'ego' or of individuality and turning it into a process of unlimited appropriation (including – perhaps most importantly – *self*-appropriation). (143)

The 'beyond of the death drive' exposes psychoanalysis to the 'other' of itself, then; a resistant other which in fact threatens to unseat the 'psychological analogy' from which new understandings of sovereign or political forms might otherwise seem to derive. That said, on closer inspection this mutation in the 'psychological analogy' may not in fact obliterate its relevance so much as restore and re-emphasize the paradoxical or perverse consequences of Freudian thought itself:

> I say that we are beyond psychologism here, but we naturally find ourselves on a very uncomfortable tightrope, as in Freud himself, between psychology and metaphysics, or between two ways, empirical or speculative, of invoking the idea of human nature. The idea of the 'death drive' and its beyond or limit can be reduced neither to Hobbes' 'war of all against all' nor to Darwin's 'natural selection' and all its applications in the political realm. (143)

Here, the death drive – never simply reducible to 'nature' (so that the 'uncomfortable tightrope' is not happened upon 'naturally'!) – itself tends to denature, distort or otherwise deconstruct all the borderlines between psychology and metaphysics, the empirical and the speculative, the 'original' and the 'historical', between natural and non-natural 'war' or 'selection', good and evil, and so on. In this sense, the death drive as much as its 'beyond' or limit already pertains to a situation in which the 'psychological analogy' that would permit 'applications in the political realm' is subjected to an altogether different logic. The normative form – that of analogy or application – which an orthodox psychologism grants is not so much dispensed with in favour of a move 'beyond' psychoanalysis itself, as it is reconstituted in a manner that is more faithful to the 'origin', if one may put it that way. To go *beyond* psychoanalysis or the death drive is in fact also to go *back* to them in the most vigilant and rigorous fashion. From this perspective, in its thinking of the modalities of violence in both their historical and contemporary cast, Balibar's Wellek lectures should be read and evaluated according to a rather complicated procedure whereby the conditions and characteristics of psychoanalytic discourse are transformed and renewed at just those moments that 'psychology' might seem to be left behind. For sure, psychoanalysis surfaces explicitly in many places throughout Balibar's lectures, but the frame of reference it makes possible is operative not only when he discusses anxiety, the Möbius strip, the mirror-stage, *object petit a* or the Real in Lacan (through which access to relevant forms of political thought is sought), but also – and perhaps precisely – where the book deals more generally with questions of sovereignty, 'life', violence and civility. This is another way of saying that psychoanalytic thought once more seems to become most powerful at the point of a certain *resistance* to itself; a resistance one might be tempted to call 'internal' since it is far from merely extrinsic, but a resistance that is nonetheless also a radically 'other' force operating within that of which it is still an essential part.

21

HANS KELSEN

POLITICS AND THE 'IMPOLITICAL'

But, bearing this in mind, let us come back to Balibar's essay
on the Freudian super-ego, which we have said represents a
crucial moment in his rethinking of the relationship between
psychoanalysis and politics. As Balibar points out, the question
of the super-ego is intrinsically connected to that of the relation
between political and psychic frames of reference, marking
thereby an original point of entry of psychoanalysis into the realm
of political thought. For Balibar, however, the Freudian concept of
the super-ego must be understood in its historical elaboration as
conditioned by a particular exchange between Freud and Hans
Kelsen, the Austrian jurist and philosopher, that happened during
this period.

As Balibar shows, Kelsen detects in Freud's work the effort to
conceptualize the State through developing the question of the
relationship between individual and society from a psychoanalytic
point of view. For Kelsen, the psychoanalytic perspective is valuable
in potentially overcoming the limits of mechanical sociological
abstractions, current at the time. However, he identifies a problem
or drawback in Freud's thinking to the extent that, from Kelsen's
standpoint, the very concept of the State inheres, as Balibar
puts it (235), 'in the positing of a *juridical norm*' that itself seems

incompatible with the modalities of psychic life on any personalized scale. Indeed, by potentially transposing the psychic dynamics of the psychoanalytic subject onto the question of political formations, Freudianism risks yolking its conception of the State to images of domination, subjection and dictatorial intent. Kelsen's reading therefore challenges Freud to acknowledge the separation of the juridical order from the particularity or indeed totality of subjective identifications, while at the same time summoning the psychoanalytic approach as potentially invaluable in maintaining the constitutional form of the State. Kelsen's dissatisfaction with a purely sociological interpretation of the juridical norm leads him, therefore, to turn to psychoanalysis as a critical supplement of legal and political philosophy. However, far from being charged with providing the explanatory apparatus linking social forms to the primordiality of psychic life, psychoanalysis is instead – through a critical reversal – perceived as the '"therapeutic" instrument of defense against the regressive archaism' (237) which threatened the democratic State, notably at this time, through fantasies or mythologies hypostatizing State omnipotence. It seems, though, that the question of the origin of these very same fantasies may reveal an intrinsically problematic or at least indupitably complex dimension in the conceptualization of the State. For if there is always the risk that subjects perceive injustices in the State, then this implies the idea of the 'juridical order as a coercive order which entails a *sanction*', in Balibar's words (237), and thus an assumption of juridical 'personality' to the extent that the State's power is thereby linked to rather anthropomorphic ideas of action and intention. To defend the State against 'regressive archaism' in the political sphere is also to recognize the aggrieved sensibilities of those who purvey such politics and hence to acknowledge, albeit perhaps unwittingly, the likely inevitability of a *motivated* conception of the State, over and above a functionalist construal of the norm. The upshot of this insight is both that Kelsen's instinct about a psychoanalytic supplement being required to rectify sociology's limits gets reinforced and that the separation of the juridical norm, on which he insists, looks to become a rather more complicated matter.

If Kelsen's reconceptualization of the practical value of psychoanalysis nonetheless challenged Freud to revise the '*antipolitical*' strain of his discourse that, in Balibar's terms, 'dissolves the specificity of all institutions within a generic "prehistory" of humanity', this led to a certain predicament: the 'citizen' form of the subject imagined by the republican jurist threatened to evacuate the psychoanalytic content of such subjectivity (even while it opened up the supplementary possibility of the complication outlined above). '*The unconscious or the political*' – for Balibar, that seemed to be the choice which Kelsen presented to Freud, notwithstanding the corrective or therapeutic value psychoanalysis might derive in addressing 'pathological representations of sovereignty' resulting from certain lapses in purely juridical conceptions of the State (239). And yet the fact that such pathologies seem to arise, historically, not just where such images of the State are inherently lacking but where they are threatened from without, as it were, itself implies that any attempt to separate the juridico-political from the 'unconscious' is inevitably complicated by the psychic reaction, akin to a subjective identification, that the 'norm' typically elicits.[1]

If such an insight seems to permit the re-implication of the 'norm' or the 'normal' and the 'pathological' – an easy win for Freud, one might imagine – nevertheless to the extent that the collaboration between Kelsen and Freud arises from broader concerns about the capacity of the constitutional State to withstand authoritarian or revolutionary challenges (Balibar emphasizes Freud's growing pessimism on this point), Freud's reaction is not just to dissolve the juridical back into the psychological, but to reframe the question of the psychoanalytic supplement of the 'political'. This involves Freud in questions of obedience, coercion and revolt. Here, however, 'the State's monopoly upon legitimate violence' is not itself psychologized, Balibar argues, as a phantasmic projection of the unconscious, which would only redouble the question of the 'political' and the 'psychic' to the point of an 'infinite regression' (241). Instead, the psychic processes involved in the reaction to State power are, in Balibar's terms, 'fundamentally *antinomial*' in character. The 'psychic tribunal' endured by the subject, in which the ego is a constant site of anxiety, recalls an analogy with the inner workings of conscience and consciousness that runs from classical conceptions of morality all the way through to Kantianism. Yet, for Balibar, Freud tests or twists this 'moral' analogy in a modern sense by effectively re-invoking the question of the norm that sanctions, in terms of the role played in such a 'tribunal' by a hypermorality that at once 'reigns in' the unconscious but also, in its very excess, surpasses distinctions between good and evil, autonomy and heteronomy, morality and law. Here we find 'the ultrajuridical authority of the super-ego' as the archetype of every real tribunal, rather than their allegorical equivalent (245). Such an 'authority' is tied to familial or collective discipline aimed not so much at prompting full identification as a certain separation and individualization. The conception of the super-ego does not therefore entail the dissolution of the 'political' into the 'psychic' but rather operates as the mechanism by which subjects are interpellated as individuals (Balibar uses this Althusserian term). The subject is not subject of a law that projects and extends a regressive psychic truth, but is instead psychically individuated, in relation to the law, on the basis of just this 'psychoanalytic' term. Where Kelsen had perhaps struggled, despite himself, to separate the juridical norm from the psychoanalytic supplement (but also to put their relations in order), Freud attempts to rework the essentially antinomial relation of psyche and law – the 'political' itself, perhaps – in a way that recovers for psychoanalysis a degree of theoretical consistency that Kelsen's writing seemed to place in doubt, while also leading to implications that cause psychoanalysis to overspill itself, if one may put it that way.

The part played by the super-ego in the 'juridical moment' of subjection involves social or structural relations whereby the connections between paternal or parental authority and political authority are not necessarily to be conceived in terms of the usual, orderly linear analogies. Instead, it is the 'ultrajuridical' authority of the super-ego that repetitively redoubles, torsions, invaginates, matricizes, or continually retransfers and turns inside out the relationships between the two – to the benefit of the forms of guilt and repression, the continual threat of punitive action, and even the onset of alienation and anomie that together subjectify individuals within grids of power. This subjectification entails not so much the collaboration of familial and social levels of authority as the persistent operation of contradictions between them. And yet the juridical order that establishes the context for this situation is only grounded on the very same conflicts that thereby threaten its decomposition as much as they secure its 'politics' – a conflictual situation, then, which is therefore continually repressed as much as it is maintained. Balibar terms this the '*impolitical*' limit or condition of the political itself.

22

SIGMUND FREUD

SUPER-EGO
POLITICS

Balibar's reading, therefore, of the evolution of a Freudian conception of the super-ego – and, crucially, its implications for an emergent psychoanalytic discourse of the 'political' – turns upon the critical reworking of this term in Freud's 1923 essay, 'The Ego and the Id'.[1] In this respect, it is important to grasp the specific set of claims that Freud wishes to set out and repeatedly underscore throughout the essay, as well as to trace the textual operations that underpin them. Certainly this text displays a degree of critical sophistication – one might better say, theoretical ambition – in its construal of the super-ego that one would perhaps struggle to find in earlier writings. First of all, on several occasions Freud is at pains to point out that the super-ego is not only an 'energetic' reaction-formation against the earliest object-choices of the id, but is also a 'residue' of them. The super-ego, in other words, constitutes itself on the strength of a situation in which ego-formation, faced with a legacy of unsatisfactory identifications arising from the id's forsaken cathexes, resorts to the supplementary agency of an ego-ideal which in fact threatens to overwhelm it, a power therefore that the ego endeavours to resist even in the context of a certain constitutive dependency upon it. Freud thus writes:

The ego is formed to a great extent out of identifications which take the place of abandoned cathexes by the id … the first of these identifications always behave as a special agency in the ego and stand apart from the ego in the form of a super-ego, while later on, as it grows stronger, the ego may become more resistant to the influences of such identifications. (48)

In other words, the super-ego arises on condition of the unresolved early conflicts of the ego with the problematic object-cathexes of the id – a conflictual situation that recourse to the super-ego not merely overcomes but also in a certain sense prolongs or exacerbates. Hence, should the ego fail to master the cathexes emanating from the id, the reaction-formation of the ego-ideal will as much resituate as resolve them on the ego's behalf. From this point of view, the the super-ego emerges not simply to help the ego overcome the id – something the ego can't manage alone – but it works instead to re-establish a connection to the unresolved concerns of the id that the ego proves itself unable to tackle by itself. Thus the super-ego is not merely an ally or counterpart in the ego's hostile relations with the id. It is, in fact, radically proximous to the id and can even act as its representative or broker *vis-à-vis* the ego. Freud goes so far as to state that the super-ego reaches deep down into the id and as such displays a greater degree of detachment from consciousness than the ego is capable of.

On several occasions, Freud tells us that the position occupied by the super-ego in the psychic field occurs on the strength of a parental dynamic characterized by Oedipal relations. On the one hand, the super-ego differentiates itself from – and seeks to dominate – the ego on the basis of an identification with a 'higher' human nature modelled on the moral position typically held by one's parents. By the same token, however, the super-ego as a reaction-formation provoked by the id's most powerful impulses is precisely the 'heir' of the Oedipus complex, 'heir' to those early conflicts of the ego with the object-cathexes of the id. The super-ego, in other words, is at once parent and child. Taking to the stage in the drama of Oedipal overcoming that the ego must perform, the super-ego serves only to reintroduce the constitutive ambivalence responsible for its own appearance on the scene. It encourages a moral identification with the father – 'you ought to be like this' – but also imposes a prohibition or repression that safeguards the limits of such identification – 'you may not be like this', 'you may not do all that he does, some things are his prerogative' (34). The ego is thus exhorted to attain maturity in the image of the parent but at the same time it is powerfully repositioned as an offspring, indeed subjected to an arresting infantilization through which Oedipal relationships are powerfully reconstituted. Thus the parent–child doublet that characterizes the ambivalent 'familial' role of the super-ego is strangely recreated in the very image of the ego, as if the unstable patterns of domination and struggle played out between them are intersected by an uncanny non-self-identical doubleness that destines their kinship relations to remain fraught and unresolved.

Freud tells us that the dread inspired in the ego by the super-ego is 'the fear of conscience' connected to the Oedipal relations that permeate their interactions (57). Here, again, the super-ego assumes a hyper-parental power while at the same time doing so through access to the legacy of an unresolved primal encounter between ego and id. Thus, one might say, the guilt inflicted upon the subject, making of them at once a conscience-following grown-up and a blameworthy adolescent, derives from the whims or caprices of an impossibly childish parent. To be fearful of 'conscience' is to know that, whether one accepts or rejects it, one loses either way. Conscience is cruel, in other words, casting its victim in an impossible predicament that in fact only reflects the cruel duplicity of the perpetrator. As Freud himself puts it:

> In all these situations the super-ego displays its independence of the conscious ego and its intimate relations with the unconscious id … From the point of view of instinctual control, of morality, it may be said of the id that it is totally non-moral, of the ego that it strives to be moral, and of the super-ego that it it can be super-moral and then become as cruel as only the id can be. (52–54)

The super-ego is at once more 'knowing' of the originary power of the unconscious than the ego might ever be, and yet at the same time, precisely to the extent that it is under the influence of the unconscious itself, such 'knowledge' must inevitably stem from what is profoundly unknowable. 'Analysis eventually shows that the super-ego is being influenced by processes that have remained unknown to the ego', writes Freud, and through this insight it becomes possible 'to discover the repressed impulses which are really at the bottom of the sense of guilt'. 'Thus in this case the super-ego knew more than the ego about the unconscious id' (51), just as psychoanalysis knows more of such matters than anyone else precisely on the strength of its unparalleled contact with unconscious forces which are themselves, nonetheless, barely susceptible to those conscious or ego-driven strategies for which the term 'knowledge' seems primarily designed. Psychoanalysis, in other words, adopts the position of the super-ego at the very moment it proclaims the possibility of such paradoxical 'knowledge' through its own conceptualization of the ego-ideal. And, again, such a gesture may appear to us at once excessively parental and extraordinarily capricious, even infantile in both its unexamined presumption and its precocious double logic. In the process, of course, Freud's claim in 'The Ego and the Id' that psychoanalysis is 'an instrument to enable the ego to achieve a progressive conquest of the id' (56) becomes deeply problematical to the extent that through its effective identification with the super-ego such analysis is just as much embroiled in the powerful impulses of the id and presumably, therefore, just as cruel 'as only the id can be'.

It is interesting, however, that during the course of his essay Freud makes explicit the analogy between analysis and its subject-matter not by drawing out the implied identity between the psychoanalyst and the super-ego, but instead through putting the 'physician' of the psyche in the position of the ego itself. The latter he describes as a 'poor creature owing service to three masters and consequently menaced by three dangers; from the external world, from the libido of the id, and from the severity of the super-ego'. On this score, one can well imagine how readily Freud might identify with such a beleaguered counterpart in trying to negotiate such complex and multiple forces or pressures. The ego, then, is presented – much like the analyst – as 'a frontier-creature' mediating between the world and the id. (Elsewhere he writes that the super-ego is constituted by relations that, in contrast to the ego's facing towards the external world, are at bottom internal to the world of the id, so that the interactions between the ego and super-ego are essentially a matter of this boundary or threshold between the two [36].) Putting psychoanalysis in the position of the ego rather than that of the super-ego obviously appeals to Freud's sense of his discipline or practice as the rational pursuit of a well-brokered relationship between the conscious and unconscious realms which inevitably weigh upon each and every individual. To the extent that such a depiction of psychoanalysis serves to ameliorate or even conceal the otherwise unfortunate connotations that may be drawn from an implied identification with the super-ego, however, the 'frontier-creature' is here as much guilty of forceful repression as felicitous conciliation. As Freud tells us, the ego is prone to repress the unconscious origin of its own guilt, and, in the case of the hysteric, the ego 'fends off a distressing perception with which the criticisms of the super-ego threaten it, in the same way in which it is in the habit of fending off an unendurable object-cathexis – by an act of repression. It is the ego, therefore, that is responsible for the sense of guilt remaining unconscious'. If this is the predicament of psychoanalysis itself, it is all the more telling that Freud continues: 'We know that as a rule the ego carries out repressions in the service and at the behest of its super-ego; but this is a case in which it has turned the same weapon against its harsh taskmaster … the ego succeeds only in keeping at a distance the material to which the sense of guilt refers' (51–52). Freud's own explicit identification with the ego thus turns out to constitute merely another maneouvre in the internecine battle with that 'harsh taskmaster' that threatens to expose its guilty secrets. In this sense, the 'truth' of psychoanalysis discloses itself once more from the perspective of the super-ego, rather than emanating from the ruses of the ego – albeit that the latter turns out to deploy exactly the same weapons as its supposed adversary.

Indeed, this drift of the ego towards the super-ego that it wants to resist – a drift brought about not least because such resistance is mounted through recourse to the rival's own amoury – leads to some rather revealing textual constructions. The ego 'behaves like the physician during an analytic treatment' in the sense that 'it offers itself, with the attention it pays to the real world, as a libidinal object to the id, and aims at attaching the id's libido to itself. It is not only a helper to the id; it is also a submissive slave who courts his master's love' (56). Drawn intimately to the super-ego through acts of courtship presumably bent on a certain yielding and consummation, such an ego becomes in the process an instrument of the id as much as its opponent. The distinction between ego and super-ego, so important in other parts of the text, here seems to erode. The ego itself begins to take on a semblance of cruelty, duplicity and immaturity that we've already identified as more characteristic of the id or the super-ego. It 'too often yields to the temptation to become sycophantic, opportunist and lying, like a politician who sees truth but wants to keep his place in popular favour' (56). The image of the ego – or, for that matter, the analyst – as a 'good' politician, a dignified and rational representative serving the interests of others from a balanced and dispassionate point of view, here quickly mutates into the inevitable corollary of the corrupt official who is guilty of lies and flattery, who is capable of bribery and intrigue, and whose respectable veneer is merely a convenient cover for rampant self-interest. This is the ego that uses the entire arsenal of its 'harsh taskmaster' to better resist their nature, only to succumb all the more deeply to it as a consequence. This is the ego with whom, as we've already suggested, Freud identifies, not fully appreciating the implications of such an act. Elsewhere, meanwhile, Freud observes that 'in the matter of action the ego's position is like that of a constitutional monarch, without whose sanction no law can be passed but who hesitates long before imposing his veto on any measure put forward by Parliament' (55). Once more, we glimpse an image of the ego's impotent sovereignty, its fading power eloquently traced in the effete figure of a puppet king dominated by forces they can barely comprehend. Lastly, by undergoing 'the attacks of the super-ego or perhaps even succumbing to them', the ego's fate is that of the 'protista' or protozoa that is 'destroyed by the products of decomposition that they themselves have created' (57). The fall from grace is complete, the ego reduced to a bare organism capable only of self-destruction.

If such a turn of events is worrisome for a psychoanalysis
that wants, however duplicitously or unadvisedly, to identify with
the ego, it also suggests consequences for the organization
of systems that are not merely natural but in several of Freud's
examples explicitly political. This brings us back, perhaps,
to Balibar's concern to weigh the political implications of the
Freudian concept of the super-ego as it develops over time
and in a variety of forms and contexts. As we saw, Kelsen's
engagement with Freud – which Balibar views as so critical in
terms of the refinement of the latter's thinking – demonstrates
Kelsen's own incapacity to entirely exclude from the juridical
conception of the state that he wishes to uphold the performative
injunction we might associate with the idea of a sanction, one
which itself causes identification on the part of the subject with
a *motivated* force or power. To the extent that this 'sanction'
appears inseparable from the workings of the juridico-political
in its state form, the psychoanalytic supplement to political
theory is not reducible merely to therapeutic inputs designed to
ameliorate regressive mythologies. Instead, the implication of
Balibar's essay is that Kelsen's intervention, in all its complexity
or equivocality, permits Freud not simply to dissolve the juridical
back into the psychological, but rather to reframe anew the
question of the psychoanalytic supplement of the political itself.
For Balibar, the subject that may be derived from this encounter
is less the subject of a law that itself embodies and extends
a regressive psychological truth, but is instead psychically
individuated in respect to the operations of a law constructed
upon deeply antinomial relations. Such relations, in other words,
function by intensifying and exploiting contradictions rather
than by promoting or enforcing analogies and correlations, in
such a way that any simplistic model tracing connections or
resemblances between certain political formations, on the one

hand, and particular psychic conditions, on the other, rather misses the point.

Whether or not the political 'figures' found in Freud's essay 'The Ego and the Id' work in such a way as to bear out this assertion, it is certainly true that the image of the super-ego that emerges from its pages may be characterized, on the one hand, as much by its detachment from the ego as by dint of patterns of identification or types of projection; while, on the other, the non-self-identical doubleness of ego and super-ego (far from the same thing as a correlative interrelationship) serves to position the ego in terms of forms of agency or sovereignty that are exposed as ineffectual, exploitable, and finally empty. While the 'sanction' of the constitutional monarch seems quite different from that of the super-ego, adding merely the weak veneer of respectability to a corrupt and manipulative political order, what lurks behind it is still the cruel power of a super-ego that the ego can barely repress, indeed which it may hold at arms length only to intensify by half-masking its insidious sway. The subject of the state 'sanction' for which the super-ego may provide a certain name is therefore not merely the citizen but ultimately the sovereign himself. It is also, of course, the psychoanalyst, whose ego-formation and self-identification turns out – if 'The Ego and the Id' is anything to go by – to confirm what Balibar calls the antinomial forces at work in the very question of a psychoanalytic supplement of politics. The intricate dynamics of this question should, we must assume, be read back into not only Freud's writings or for that matter his exchanges with interlocutors and contemporaries like Kelsen, but they must surely also condition any effort to weigh the legacy and value of psychoanalytic thought from a political perspective (including the attempt by Balibar himself). For Melanie Klein, the shift from the paranoid-schizoid to the depressive position in the journey of ego-formation was thought to lessen the severity of a super-ego not contingent as in Freud upon the primacy of Oedipal relations. For Lacan, certainly insofar as authors like Slavoj Žižek are concerned, the super-ego forces us to betray the law of desire, demanding *jouissance* as nothing but a violent and traumatic intrusion which causes more pain than pleasure, notably since the betrayal it imposes on us constitutes the actual origin or explanation for our guilt. However, various attempts within the field of psychoanalysis to refine or rework the concept of the super-ego are surely just as much subject to the question of this psycho-political dynamic. It is one that asks not merely about the 'psychic' conditions of politics, but also the 'politics' of psychologizing discourse in all its forms. And let us remember, its 'double' effects – if past results are anything to go by – are likely to be as much antinomial and divisive as they may be instructive and empowering.

And yet, at the frontier of politics and psychoanalysis as much as anywhere else, there is the 'leap of decision' to which Derrida alludes in *Politics of Friendship*. A leap which, by forgoing established knowledge or 'theoretical or reportive determination', as Derrida puts it, resembles just those leaps imagined by writers as diverse as Arendt, Blanchot, Benjamin and Klein, ones we have traced throughout this book. A leap that, as Vincent B. Leitch has written, cannot ignore the complexities that weigh upon it, but which must indeed 'bear antinomies and double binds'.[2]

NOTES

Hope Against Hope

1 Slavoj Žižek, *The Courage of Hopelessness: Chronicles of a Year of Acting Dangerously* (London: Allen Lane, 2017), xxi. Further page references are given in the body of my introduction.

2 Several recent analyses of contemporary theoretical, cultural or political issues have drawn on the language and discourse either of optimism or pessimism. See, for example, Lauren Berlant's *Cruel Optimism* (Durham, NC: Duke University Press, 2011), mentioned in my introduction, and Michael D. Snediker, *Queer Optimism* (Minneapolis: University of Minnesota Press, 2008). For other examples on this topic, see also Joshua Dienstag, *Pessimism: Philosophy, Ethic, Spirit* (Princeton, NJ: Princeton University Press, 2006) and Stuart Sim, *A Philosophy of Pessimism* (London: Reaktion, 2015).

3 Giorgio Agamben, 'Thought is the courage of hopelessness', interview with Jordan Skinner, 17 June 2014, available at https://www.versobooks.com/blogs/1612-thought-is-the-courage-of-hopelessness-an-interview-with-philosopher-giorgio-agamben.

4 Walter Benjamin, 'Surrealism: The Last Snapshot of the European Intelligentsia', trans. Edmond Jephcott, *New Left Review* 108 (1978). Note that this and other texts cited throughout the remainder of this introduction relate to material that is discussed in more detail in the ensuing sections of the book, with relevant page references given as necessary.

5 Theodor Adorno, *Minima Moralia: Reflections from Damaged Life*, trans. E. F. N. Jephcott (London and New York: Verso, 2005).

6 Berlant, *Cruel Optimism*, 3.

7 Another interesting recent text in regard to this topic is Eugene Thacker, *Infinite Resignation: On Pessimism* (London: Repeater, 2018).

8   See my account of Arendt's *The Promise of Politics* in Chapter 4.

9   Benedict de Spinoza, *Theological-Political Treatise*, ed. Jonathan
        Israel, trans. Michael Silverthorne and Jonathan Israel (Cambridge:
        Cambridge University Press, 2007–08)

10   Immanuel Kant, 'An Attempt at Some Reflections on Optimism', in
        *The Cambridge Edition of the Works of Immanuel Kant: Theoretical
        Philosophy 1755–1770*, ed. and trans. David Walford (Cambridge:
        Cambridge University Press, 2007).

11   Voltaire, *Candide, or Optimism*, trans. Theo Cuffe (London:
        Penguin, 2005).

12   Arthur Schopenhauer, 'On the Sufferings of the World', in *Studies in
        Pessimism* (Sittard: Diderot Publishing, 2017), 13.

13   Friedrich Nietzsche, *The Will to Power: Selections from the
        Notebooks of the 1880s*, trans. R. Kevin Hill and Michael A.
        Scarpitti, ed. R. Kevin Hill (London: Penguin, 2017).

14   Maurice Blanchot, 'Reflections on Nihilism', in *The Infinite
        Conversation*, trans. Susan Hanson (Minneapolis and London:
        Minnesota University Press, 1993).

15   Jacques Derrida, 'A Number of Yes', in *Psyche: Inventions of
        the Other, Volume II*, ed. Peggy Kamuf and Elizabeth Rottenberg
        (Stanford, CA: Stanford University Press, 2008).

16   Emmanuel Levinas, *Time and the Other*, trans. Richard A. Cohen
        (Pittsburgh, PA: Duquesne University Press, 1987).

17   As I suggest later in the book, in the mid-twentieth century (during
        and after the war), something of this thought is to be found in
        Adorno as much as Levinas.

18   Sigmund Freud, 'Analysis Terminable and Interminable', in *The
        Complete Psychological Works of Sigmund Freud* Vol. XXIII, ed. and
        trans. James Strachey (London: Vintage, 2001).

19   Julia Kristeva, *Melanie Klein*, trans. Ross Guberman (New York:
        Columbia University Press, 2001).

20   Julia Kristeva, *Black Sun: Depression and Melancholia*, trans. Leon
        S. Roudiez (New York, Columbia University Press, 1989).

21 Étienne Balibar, 'The Invention of the Super-Ego: Freud and Kelsen, 1922', in *Citizen Subject; Foundations for Philosophical Anthropology*, trans. Steven Miller (New York: Fordham University Press, 2017).

22 Hannah Arendt, 'Reflections on Violence', in *The New York Review of Books* 12.4 (27 February 1969).

23 I do think 'hope against hope' entails a different proposition from that of Žižek's hopeless courage, which as I suggest is inevitably just a little hopeless at hopelessness. I trust the present study makes it clear that I think hopelessness is never really an option, so that – if one is perhaps inevitably dissatisfied with hope itself – one must nevertheless speculate on 'hope' differently, rather than just seeking to abandon it altogether.

24 Maurice Blanchot, 'The Great Refusal', in *The Infinite Conversation*, trans. Susan Hanson (Minneapolis and London: Minnesota University Press, 1993).

25 Hannah Arendt, *The Promise of Politics*, ed. Jerome Kohn (New York: Schocken Books, 2005).

26 Walter Benjamin, 'Franz Kafka: On the Tenth Anniversary of his Death', in *Illuminations*, ed. Hannah Arendt, trans. Harry Zorn (London: Pimlico, 1999).

27 See also the concluding chapter and especially the last paragraph of this book.

Chapter 1

1 Immanuel Kant, 'An Attempt at Some Reflections on Optimism', in *The Cambridge Edition of the Works of Immanuel Kant: Theoretical Philosophy 1755–1770*, ed. and trans. David Walford (Cambridge: Cambridge University Press, 2007), 67–76. Further references to this text and appended matter also included in this volume are given in the main body of the chapter.

Chapter 2

1 All references are to Voltaire, *Philosophical Dictionary*, ed. and trans. Theodore Besterman (London: Penguin, 1972).
2 Voltaire, *Candide, or Optimism*, trans. Theo Cuffe (London: Penguin, 2005).

Chapter 3

1 Arthur Schopenhauer, 'On the Sufferings of the World', in *Studies in Pessimism* (Sittard: Diderot Publishing, 2017). Further page references are given in the body of the chapter.
2 All references are to Arthur Schopenhauer, *The World as Will and Representation*, Volume I, trans. E.F.J. Payne (New York: Dover Publications, 1966).
3 If 'all is good', as the optimist proposes, then why, as Schopenhauer asks elsewhere, is any momentary cessation of will characterized by miserable, unrelieved boredom?
4 All references are to Arthur Schopenhauer, *The World as Will and Representation*, Volume II, trans. E.F.J. Payne (New York: Dover Publications, 1969).

Chapter 4

1 Benedict de Spinoza, *Theological-Political Treatise*, ed. Jonathan Israel (Cambridge: Cambridge University Press, 2007). Page reference are given in the body of the chapter.

Chapter 5

1 Friedrich Nietzsche, *The Will to Power: Selections from the Notebooks of the 1880s*, trans. R. Kevin Hill and Michael A. Scarpitti,

ed. R. Kevin Hill (London: Penguin, 2017). Page references are given in the main body of the text.

2 Maurice Blanchot, 'Reflections on Nihilism', in *The Infinite Conversation*, trans. Susan Hanson (Minneapolis and London: Minnesota University Press, 1993), 136–70. Page references are given in the main body of the text.

Chapter 6

1 Maurice Blanchot, 'The Great Refusal', in *The Infinite Conversation*, 33–48. Further page references are given in the body of this section.

Chapter 7

1 All references are to Jacques Derrida, 'A Number of Yes', in *Psyche: Inventions of the Other, Volume II*, ed. Peggy Kamuf and Elizabeth Rottenberg (Stanford, CA: Stanford University Press, 2008), 231–40.

2 Jacques Derrida, 'Ulysses Gramophone: Hear Say Yes in Joyce', trans. Tina Kendall and Shari Benstock, in *James Joyce: The Augmented Ninth*, ed. Bernard Benstock (Syracuse: Syracuse University Press, 1988), 27–75.

3 Giorgio Agamben, 'Thought Is the Courage of Hopelessness', interview with Jordan Skinner, 17 June 2014, available at https://www.versobooks.com/blogs/1612-thought-is-the-courage-of-hopelessness-an-interview-with-philosopher-giorgio-agamben. This interview is further discussed elsewhere in the book.

Chapter 8

1 Emmanuel Levinas, *Time and the Other*, trans. Richard A. Cohen (Pittsburgh, PA: Duquesne University Press, 1987). Page references are given in the main body of the chapter.

2 Levinas writes here: 'It is impersonal like "it is raining" or "it is hot"'.

3 This term is explicitly connected, by Levinas, to the identity and self-definition of 'optimistic', constructivist 'sociology and socialism' (61).

4 See, for instance, Steven Hendley, *From Communicative Action to the Face of the Other: Levinas and Habermas on Language, Obligation, and Community* (New York: Lexington Books, 2000), 116.

5 See Levinas's 1984 interview with Salomon Malka, included in the collection *Is It Righteous to Be? Interviews with Emmanuel Levinas*, ed. Jill Robbins (Stanford, CA: Stanford University Press, 2001), 93–104, where Levinas protests just this description of his work. He further refuses the choice between optimism and pessimism as viable alternatives that may establish any kind of ground for philosophical judgements.

Chapter 9

1 See Sigmund Freud, 'Analysis Terminable and Interminable', in *The Complete Psychological Works of Sigmund Freud*, Vol. XXIII, ed. and trans. James Strachey (London: Vintage, 2001), 216–54. Page references are given in the body of the chapter.

2 Later on in the essay, with not inconsiderable pessimism concerning this style of warfare, Freud writes that 'analysis can only draw upon definite and limited amounts of energy which have to be measured against the hostile forces. And it seems as if victory is in fact as a rule on the side of the big battalions' (240).

3 Like the suicidal jihadist, perhaps.

Chapter 10

1 All references in this section of the chapter are to Julia Kristeva, *Melanie Klein* (New York: Columbia University Press, 2001).

Chapter 11

1 All references here are to Julia Kristeva, *Black Sun: Depression and Melancholia*, trans. Leon S. Roudiez (New York: Columbia University Press, 1989).

Chapter 12

1 Walter Benjamin, 'Surrealism: the Last Snapshot of the European Intelligentsia', trans. Edmond Jephcott, *New Left Review* 108 (1978), 47–56. Specific page references are given in the body of my chapter.

Chapter 13

1 See Theodor Adorno, *Minima Moralia: Reflections from Damaged Life* (London and New York: Verso, 2005). Page references are given in the body of the chapter.
2 Elsewhere in the text, Adorno writes that 'the value of a thought is measured by its distance from the familiar', so that authentic intellectual production in precisely its 'antithetical function' jettisons the 'liberal fiction' of 'universal communicability' (80) that matches the unjust sociability critiqued by Adorno.

Chapter 14

1 Hannah Arendt, *The Promise of Politics*, ed. Jerome Kohn (New York: Schocken Books, 2005), 93–200. Page references are given in the main body of the chapter.

Chapter 15

1 Slavoj Žižek, *The Courage of Hopelessness: Chronicles of a Year of Acting Dangerously* (London: Allen Lane, 2017).

2 Giorgio Agamben, 'Thought Is the Courage of Hopelessness', interview with Jordan Skinner, 17 June 2014, available at https://www.versobooks.com/blogs/1612-thought-is-the-courage-of-hopelessness-an-interview-with-philosopher-giorgio-agamben.

3 G. W. F. Hegel, *Outlines of the Philosophy of Right*, trans. T. M. Knox (Oxford: Oxford University Press, 2008). Page references are in the body of my chapter.

4 Alain Badiou, 'Le courage du présent', *Le Monde*, 13 February 2010. English translation (cited here) available online at http://www.lacan.com/symptom11/the-courage.html.

5 If in Hegel's *Philosophy of Right* the only ends worthy of the name are, as it were, dead ends, implying the radical demise of individual 'life' as such, for Badiou the contemporary present tasks us to overcome dead ends, albeit in a different sense (although, given my analysis, not an entirely unconnected one).

Chapter 16

1 Walter Benjamin, 'Franz Kafka: On the Tenth Anniversary of His Death', in *Illuminations*, ed. Hannah Arendt, trans. Harry Zorn (London: Pimlico, 1999), 108–35. Page references are given in the body of the chapter.

2 Peter Fenves, *Arresting Language: From Leibniz to Benjamin* (Stanford, CA: Stanford University Press, 2002). References are given in the body of the chapter.

3 It should not be assumed, however, that there is any signature without some degree of fraudulence, any more than there is any narrative that is not somewhat anecdotal, or for that matter any hope that is free of every taint of self-interest.

Chapter 17

1 Jacques Derrida, 'From Restricted to General Economy: A
   Hegelianism without Reserve', in *Writing and Difference*, trans. Alan
   Bass (London: Routledge, 1990), 251–77. Specific page references
   are given in the body of the chapter.
2 However, this generally chronological structure itself throws up
   interesting questions, for instance whether date of publication, date
   of public presentation or date of authorship was the key factor in
   deciding running order, how strictly the schema was applied and
   what the criteria for exceptions might have been (thematic continuity,
   intellectual progression, cognate subject-matter?). For our purposes
   in particular, one wonders why the essay on Hegel and Bataille – other
   than the specially written end-piece, the only text in the collection to
   appear in its own right in 1967 – does not close the show, that honour
   going instead to the much more famous and influential talk from the
   1966 Baltimore conference at Johns Hopkins, 'Structure, Sign and
   Play in the Discourse of the Human Sciences', which greatly helped
   establish Derrida's reputation in the Anglo-American academy. Since
   Derrida did not substantially return to or expand his reading of Bataille,
   one wonders about the status of this piece in Derrida's own mind, and
   whether that was a factor in its positioning in the volume.
3 Since, as Derrida remarks, servility is really 'only the desire for
   meaning' (262), the lordly master is as servile, if not more so, than the
   lowest slave.

Chapter 18

1 Fanon's *The Wretched of the Earth* had been translated into English
   earlier in the 1960s, and for a time carried an introduction by Jean-
   Paul Sartre, until it was removed on the instruction of Fanon's widow,
   who objected to Sartre's position on Israel notably in the context of
   the Arab–Israeli war of 1967.

2 Examples include David Caute's biography, *Fanon*, for the Fontana
Modern Masters series edited by Frank Kermode (London: Fontana,
1970) and Peter Geismar's *Fanon: The Revolutionary as Prophet*
(New York: Dial Press, 1971). In 1969, of course, Hannah Arendt
published her famous piece, 'Reflections on Violence' in *The New
York Review of Books* 12, 4 (27 February 1969).

3 In Frantz Fanon, *Black Skin, White Masks*, trans. Charles Lam
Markmann (London: Pluto Press, 1993). Page references are given in
the body of the text.

4 For Homi Bhabha, writing of *Black Skin, White Masks* in his 'Foreword'
to the English edition, 'recognition' in its Hegelian sense 'fails to ignite
in the colonial relation where there is only narcissistic indifference' (xxi);
in other words, where the colonized's desire for recognition-through-
struggle is met with an historic evasion of this very desire.

5 This recognition (along with my broader suggestion concerning an
'imperfect dialectics' at work in Fanon's writings) perhaps resonates
productively with Homi Bhabha's assertion, in his 'Foreword'
to *Black Skin, White Masks*, that Fanon 'may yearn for the total
transformation of Man and Society, but he speaks most effectively
from the uncertain interstices of historical change… To read Fanon
is to experience the sense of division that prefigures – and fissures –
the emergence of a truly radical thought that never dawns without
casting an uncertain dark' (ix).

6 As is well known, Fanon supplements Merleau-Ponty's
phenomenological account of embodiment in the world by developing
an epidermal historico-racial analysis as a critical rejoinder to what
may be seen as Merleau-Ponty's overly inclusive corporeal schema.

Chapter 19

1 Hannah Arendt, 'Reflections on Violence', *The New York Review of
Books*, 27 February 1969, available online: https://www.nybooks.com/
articles/1969/02/27/a-special-supplement-reflections-on-violence/.

2 Arendt on a number of occasions also takes issue with the speculative
optimism of dialectical thought post-Hegel and Marx.

3 Arendt writes of the question, 'What is the end of government?' that it 'does not make much sense … The answer will be either question-begging – to enable men to live together – or dangerously utopian: to promote happiness or to realize a classless society or some other nonpolitical ideal, which if tried out in earnest can only end in the worst kind of government, that is, tyranny'.

4 For Arendt, the substitution of violence for power often leads politically to a situation of terror, from which the master himself is not exempt. Thus, for instance, totalitarian regimes often become not merely repressive but self-destructive at their very centre.

5 Here, Fanon is described merely as more intimately experienced in relation to practices of violence than other of its glorifiers.

Chapter 20

1 Étienne Balibar, 'The Invention of the Super-Ego: Freud and Kelsen, 1922', in *Citizen Subject; Foundations for Philosophical Anthropology*, trans. Steven Miller with a Foreword by Emily Apter (New York: Fordham University Press, 2017), 227–55. Where relevant, page references are given in the main body of my essay. As well as the text on Freud, this volume includes essays on Descartes, Locke, Rousseau, Hegel, Marx, Blanchot, Benveniste, Derrida and Nancy, connected to its major themes.

2 Étienne Balibar, *Violence and Civility: On the Limits of Political Philosophy*, trans. G. M. Goshgarian (New York: Columbia University Press, 2015). Where relevant, page references are given in the main body of my essay.

3 See, for instance, 'Outline of a Topography of Cruelty: Citizenship and Civility in the Era of Global Violence', included in Balibar's *We, the People of Europe?: Reflections on Transnational Citizenship* (Princeton, NJ: Princeton University Press, 2003), 115–32, esp. 121ff. Further page references to this text are given in the main body of the chapter.

4 Drawing on Wendy Brown's 'Neoliberalism and the End of Liberal Democracy', in *Edgework: Critical Essays on Knowledge and Politics* (Princeton, NJ: Princeton University Press, 2005), 37–59, Balibar offers some commentary on this topic in his own essay, 'Antinomies

of Citizenship', *Journal of Romance Studies* 10, 2 (2010): 1–20; this
material also forms the introduction to Balibar's *Equaliberty: Political
Essays* (Durham, NC and London: Duke University Press, 2014),
1–32.

Chapter 21

1   Later in the same essay, Balibar writes of Kelsen's conception of
the juridical norm as coercive, and as such based on an ideological
legitimization of State violence over non-State violence: 'An order
defined in such a manner possesses an absolute character, since it
isn't possible to get outside of it or legitimately to resist it. I believe,
more precisely, that according to Kelsen, such an order forms a
fiction of the absolute in the mode of an "as if", since it entirely
depends on the *institutional supposition* of the juridical, obligatory,
and coercive character of the "fundamental norm" that grounds
it. This is the very point at which the Freudian reversal… would
intervene' (254).

Chapter 22

1   Sigmund Freud, 'The Ego and the Id', in *The Standard Edition of
the Complete Psychological Works of Sigmund Freud*, Volume XIX
(1923–1925), translated under the general editorship of James
Strachey (London: Vintage, 2001), 12–66. Where relevant, page
references are given in the main body of my essay.
2   Vincent B. Leitch, 'Late Derrida: The Politics of Sovereignty', *Critical
Inquiry* 33, 2 (2007), 229–47: 239. Leitch quotes from *Politics of
Friendship*, trans. George Collins (London: Verso, 1997), 219, where
Derrida himself writes that such leaps of decision 'may and must be
preceded by all possible science and conscience', so that from a
deconstructive perspective we might presume the leap's very milieu
is the antinomial. (In his essay 'Mochlos', writing on Kant, Derrida

tells us that in order to make the leap each foot somehow has to support the other; however, to exert the necessary leverage involves the advent of a certain alterity or heterogeneity in precisely the midst of such double 'support'. On this theme, see my own 'Van Gogh's Shoes, or, Does the University Have Two Left Feet?', in *Rethinking the University: Leverage and Deconstruction* (Manchester: Manchester University Press, 1999), 21–48. One might also discuss the leap in Heidegger's 'The Origin of the Work of Art', also discussed in my chapter cited above (Catherine Malabou explores the Heideggerian leap more generally throughout *The Heidegger Change: On the Fantastic in Philosophy* [New York: SUNY Press, 2011]). See also the qualitative leap or leap of faith in Kierkegaard, or for that matter Marx's use of 'Hic Rhodus, hic salta!' In the *Eighteenth Brumaire*.)

INDEX

Abraham, Karl 77
action 10, 72, 81, 84, 86, 90,
    92–3, 99, 109, 126–7, 130–1,
    140, 151
Adler, Alfred 118
Adorno, Theodor 2–3, 8, 84–8
affirmation 7–8, 11, 39–43, 45–8,
    56, 100, 114, 123, 125
Agamben, Giorgio 2, 47, 97–8
Althusser, Louis 142
anarchism 36–7, 83
anecdote 103–7
animal 26–7, 92, 99
Arendt, Hannah 4, 10–11, 72,
    89–93, 109–10, 125–31, 154
Aristotle 76

Badiou, Alain viii, 100–2, 162
Balibar, Étienne 10, 133–6,
    138–43, 145, 152–3
Bataille, Georges 110–14,
    117–18, 120–1, 129, 131
Benjamin, Walter 2, 8, 11, 81–4,
    103–5, 107, 154
Berlant, Lauren 3–4
Blanchot, Maurice 7, 11, 38–9,
    41–4, 154
Bolingbroke, Henry St John 1st
    Viscount 23

Bonnefoy, Yves 43
bourgeois 2, 82–3, 86, 88, 97
Brexit 95

capitalism 1, 84–5, 134
Char, René 42
Charcot, Jean-Martin 133
China 1, 102
Christian 28, 35, 37, 46
citizen 134–5, 141, 153
colonial 117–18, 120–1, 125, 129
communism 84, 100–2
consciousness 51, 85, 101,
    111–12, 118–20, 122, 142,
    146, 148–9
courage 2–3, 97–100, 102
cruelty 135, 151

Darwin, Charles 137
death 8, 42, 53–4, 56, 69, 71–3,
    77–9, 111–12, 130, 136
death drive 72–3, 135–7
de Certeau, Michel 7, 45–7
decision 48–9, 66, 95, 113, 154
deconstruction 10, 48, 110–11,
    120–1, 129, 137
democracy 48–9, 134, 140
depression 75–9
depressive state 71, 74, 78, 153

Derrida, Jacques 7, 10, 42, 45–9, 109–15, 117–18, 120–1, 129, 131, 136, 154

desire 18, 32, 39, 41–2, 44, 71–4, 96, 107, 113, 118–19, 122, 126, 154

despair 4, 9, 22, 28, 48, 55, 64, 68, 76–9, 96, 107

dialectics 38, 55, 72, 82–4, 110, 112–14, 120, 122

dilettantism 2, 36, 82

Dostoevsky, Fyodor 82

ego 63, 65, 71, 73–4, 136, 142, 145–53

Enlightenment 4–5, 15, 20–2, 29, 86

Epicurus 22

Eros 71, 78–9

Europe 1, 5–6, 9, 15, 21, 37, 60, 66, 95, 122, 134

evil 5, 16, 18–19, 22–5, 35, 82, 136–7, 142

existentialism 55

faith 5, 30–3, 35, 92

Fanon, Frantz 10, 109–10, 117–18, 120–3, 125–7, 129–31

fascism 135

fear 5, 29–33, 71–2, 89–91, 93, 147

Fenves, Peter 103–4

Foucault, Michel 128

Freud, Sigmund 8–10, 59–69, 71–3, 77, 133, 135–7, 139–43, 145–54

future viii, 9, 42–3, 47–9, 54, 62–6, 69, 88, 100, 130

German Romanticism 81

global 1, 4, 95, 134

guilt 35, 77, 96, 123, 143, 147–8, 150–1, 154

Hegel, Georg Wilhelm Friedrich 3, 10, 84, 99–102, 109–14, 117–22, 129–31

Heidegger, Martin 47

Hobbes, Thomas 137

hope viii, 2–6, 9–11, 16, 19–20, 22, 24, 27–30, 32–3, 41–3, 48, 55, 60, 64–5, 67, 74, 83–4, 86–93, 96–102, 105, 107–8

hopeless 2–3, 6, 28, 36, 93, 97–8, 100, 102, 108

id 145–51

impolitical 143

impossible 7, 31, 39, 41–4, 48, 53–4, 63, 68, 96, 101–2, 107–8, 123, 125, 147–8

individual 18, 31, 59, 64, 86–7, 99–100, 130, 136, 139, 142–3

Jewish 46

Joyce, James 46

judgement 5, 29–33, 92

juridical norm 139–43, 152

Kafka, Franz 11, 103, 105, 107

Kant, Immanuel 5, 15–19, 23–4, 78, 93, 142

Keslen, Hans 10, 139–43, 152–3

Klein, Melanie 9, 11, 71–4, 77–8

Kristeva, Julia 9, 71–9

Lacan, Jacques 138
Lactantius Firmianus 22
laughter 112
leap 11, 88, 154
left 2–5, 8, 82–6, 97, 126–7
Leibniz, Gottfried Wilhelm 5,
    17–19, 22–5, 27, 35
Leitch, Vincent B. 154
Le Monde 100
Lessing, Gotthold Ephraim
    15–16
Levinas, Emmanuel 8, 51–7, 62, 85
life 27–9, 36, 43–4, 53, 71–4,
    91–2, 111–13, 119, 122, 130,
    136, 138, 140
linguistics 45, 110
Lisbon earthquake 16
lordship 110–13, 115, 118, 123,
    129

Mao Zedong 102
Marx, Karl 84, 89, 98
Marxism 55, 89, 118, 126–7
mastery 41, 51, 53, 107, 110,
    111, 115, 118–22, 128–30,
    146, 149, 150
melancholy 75–6, 78
Mendelssohn, Moses 15–16
metaphysics 16, 77, 84, 87,
    110–11, 113, 137
miracle 11, 91–3
mysticism 81, 83

Naville, Pierre 83
negativity 7, 26, 39, 41–3, 45,
    47–8, 73–4, 112–13
Nerval, Gérard de 78
The New York Review of Books
    10, 109, 125

Nietzsche, Friedrich 6–8, 35–9,
    41–2, 46, 84, 87
nihilism 6–7, 35–42, 48
nuclear 65–6, 89, 91

object 1, 41, 52, 71–3, 76–9,
    81, 83, 92, 118, 138, 145–7,
    150
Oedipus complex 146–7, 154
optimism 2–6, 8–9, 11, 15–29,
    35–6, 47–8, 55–7, 60–2,
    64–6, 69, 74, 82–7, 98, 100

paranoid-schizoid state 71, 153
party 86–7
pessimism 2–4, 6–11, 20, 22, 24,
    28, 35–8, 47–8, 56–7, 62–5,
    68–9, 73–4, 76, 79, 83–4,
    97–8, 100, 107, 141
phenomenology 46, 55
Plato 54, 113
poetry 11, 42–4
politics 1–4, 7–8, 10–11, 17–18,
    49, 55, 57, 65, 81–4, 86–7,
    89–93, 95, 97, 109, 118,
    126–7, 130–1, 133–5,
    137–43, 145, 151–4
Pope, Alexander 15–16, 18–20,
    23, 27
populism 1, 4, 95
power 7, 10, 23–4, 39, 51, 63,
    65–6, 68, 86, 90–1, 104–6,
    109–10, 126–30, 138, 140,
    142–3, 145, 147–9, 151–3
Prussian Royal Academy 15, 19
psychoanalysis 8–11, 59, 62–6,
    68–9, 71–2, 74–7, 79, 118,
    133, 135–43, 145, 148–50,
    152–4

psychology 6, 35, 96, 118, 133,
   136–8, 142, 152, 154
Putin, Vladimir 95

Rank, Otto 59–61
recognition 112, 115, 117–22
Reinhard, Adolf Friedrich von 15–16
resistance 3–4, 6–8, 10, 22,
   41–2, 59, 62, 64–5, 68–9, 85,
   90, 98, 101, 104–5, 109, 118,
   121–2, 126, 129–31, 135–6,
   138, 145–6, 150–1
revolution 2, 4, 21, 24, 81–4,
   97–9, 101–2, 105, 117,
   125–8, 141
Rimbaud, Arthur 82

Sartre, Jean-Paul 126
Schlechta, Karl 38
Schopenhauer, Arthur 6, 25–8
Shaftesbury, 3rd Earl of (Anthony
   Ashley-Cooper) 15, 23
signature 46, 104–6
Skinner, Jordan 97
slave 107, 110–12, 119–22, 129,
   150
smoking 2, 95–7
socialism 38, 55, 62, 87
sociality 8, 55–6, 86, 91
sociology 55, 62, 139–41
solidarity 3, 8, 55, 86–7
solitude 8, 51–3, 55–7
sovereignty 31, 99–100, 108,
   111–15, 120–1, 129–30,
   136–8, 141, 151, 153
Spinoza, Benedict de 5, 29–33
state 31–2, 48–9, 90–1, 99–100,
   105–7, 130, 134–6, 139–42,
   152–3

Strachey, James 59
structuralism 110, 143
suffering 5–6, 21–2, 24–8, 53–6,
   63, 67–9, 82
super-ego 10, 133, 139, 142–3,
   145–54
surrealism 2, 81–4
Svevo, Italo 95, 101

terrorism 1, 67, 95, 135
Thanatos 71, 78–9
theodicy 6, 22, 24, 82, 86
theology 31, 46, 84, 87
therapy 9, 59–60, 62, 68–9,
   72–4, 76, 79, 140–1, 152
Trump, Donald 3–4, 95

unconscious 71–3, 141–2,
   148–50
United States 2, 86, 109, 117,
   134
utopia 42, 48, 90

violence 10–11, 67, 73, 84, 86,
   109–10, 115, 122–3, 125–31,
   135–6, 138, 142, 154
Voltaire 5–6, 16, 21–4, 27–8

war 2, 9, 21, 51, 60–1, 66–7, 69,
   85, 89–93, 102, 121, 127,
   137
Weil, Simone 43
Weyman, Daniel 16
workers' movement 2, 85

yes 7, 40–1, 45–8

Žižek, Slavoj 1–2, 95, 97–8,
   101–2, 154